What others are s[...]
Make Your Golf Drea[...]

Want to improve quickly? Read this book. It's good "fore" you. – **Todd Hamilton, 2004 British Open Champion.**

I have known Lou Hays and played golf with him for several years. He definitely lives by the words he writes. The ideas of "Make Your Golf Dream a Reality" have improved my short game and enabled me to win the Cherry Cup Classic two out of the past four years. Lou writes simply and understandably. But most importantly, what he says, works. You could read scores of golf instruction books (as I have) and not be helped as much as by reading this one. I highly recommend it to any golfer who loves (and hates) the game as much as we do. – **Bob Batson, scratch golfer.**

I thought I had recovered completely from Golf Fever, but after reading this book, that pesky old voice is saying "I can do this!" These are some of the easiest-to-understand explanations I have seen, and the author really does create enthusiasm. – **Rebecca A. Williamson, amateur golfer.**

"Make Your Golf Dream a Reality" is a must read and ongoing reference. Distance control (Chapter 7) has stuck with me over time. Thanks Lou! – **John Della Maggiora, amateur golfer having more fun with less frustration.**

Tips to improve the short game really do work and they're simple to understand and apply. I especially like the "eight-iron putt" and using my sand wedge on something other than a bunker shot. With a little practice, I expect my game will continue to improve. – **Bill Clark, a 90's duffer, moving into the 80's.**

MAKE YOUR GOLF DREAM A REALITY

MAKE YOUR GOLF DREAM A REALITY

Realistic Techniques for Reaching Your Golf Goals (in Record Time!)

Lou Hays

Hays Publishing
Park Hill, Oklahoma

ISBN 1-880673-77-0

Printed in the United States of America
1   3   5   7   9   10   8   6   4   2

Dedicated to my dear friend Zola Levitt (1938-2006),
who first said, "Lou, let's go play golf!"

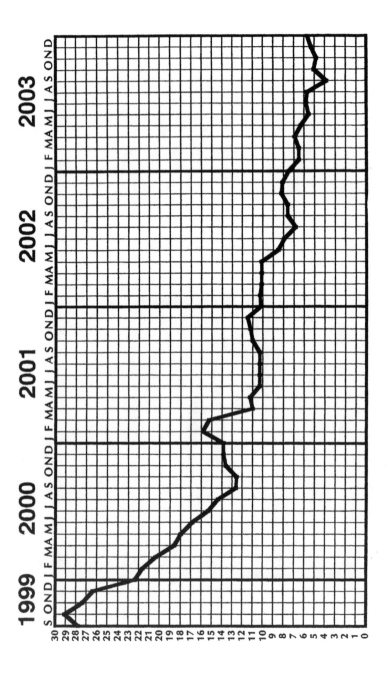

Charting My Handicap, Early Years

CONTENTS

Foreword

One summer day a number of years ago, the author of this book, Lou Hays, showed up at Cherry Springs Golf Course in Tahlequah, Oklahoma, where I was the head professional. He was a new golfer seeking lessons and he appeared to be highly motivated.

I have given thousands of golf lessons in the eighteen years since I became a professional and my greatest pleasure has come not from the money I've earned teaching, but from watching my students develop into accomplished golfers. For that reason, my experience teaching Lou was particularly gratifying.

From the beginning, he was painstakingly appraising his game and working to surmount the mistakes blocking his improvement. During that first year, whenever he'd show up for a lesson, he would bring with him a definite problem that he couldn't work out on his own. We'd go to the range, practice green, or bunker and resolve the trouble, usually in an hour or less.

A year after he started playing, I left Cherry Springs and became Director of Golf at the Pryor (OK) Golf Course, about an hour's drive from Lou's home. Although I didn't see him nearly as often, I'd still get the occasional anxious call when he was stymied by some problem that had cropped up in his game. He'd dash up to Pryor, we'd work through the trouble, and he'd be on his happy way.

My teaching and his efforts paid off. Before long he had achieved a low single-digit handicap and was competing in state championship tournaments.

As the years passed, Lou became sympathetic to the plight of high handicap golfers. He saw them ruining their scores (and fun) with the same grievous errors that he had experienced and dealt with in his own game. He could certainly relate to these golfers' lack of ability to understand the causes of their high scores. He wanted to help, but realized that unsolicited advice on the golf course is impolite at best and dangerous at worst.

Lou has been a book publisher for many years, so a golf book became the logical vehicle for sharing his story and conveying his ideas. In 2005 he confided that he had begun work on a book outlining the process that had worked so well for him. In the book he hoped to help struggling golfers learn to understand the causes of their difficulties and to reveal the techniques he had so successfully applied to his own game. A year or so later he sent sample books to me and several other golf pros for review and comment. You hold in your hands the end result of those efforts.

You will find in these pages a wealth of sound and practical ideas you can use to immediately start improving your golf scores. Unlike golf books that concentrate on how to swing a golf club, *Make Your Golf Dream a Reality* is about examining your game and getting the most out of the assets you already possess. You'll stop wasting time practicing in a way that won't advance your game and instead learn how to quickly drop your scores and handicap with organized and well-planned effort.

I have carefully evaluated the contents of this book and find the lessons not only sound, but essential steps to the progress of anyone seeking improvement, particularly those golfers with limited time for practice. The instructions come in a logical, easy-to-follow format and flow in a straightforward and engaging style.

Add to this a sincere desire to improve and you'll reach your own golf goals sooner than you believe possible.

Dennis Bowman
PGA Professional
Cobblestone Creek Golf Course, Muskogee, Oklahoma
Pryor Golf Course, Pryor, Oklahoma

Introduction

If you truly desire to improve your golf game, you're going to love this book. It's designed to make you understand, once and for all, the real reasons you continue to shoot fifteen to fifty shots over par. It will teach you to look at golf improvement in an entirely different way. **The book systematically addresses classic high handicapper mistakes and reveals surefire ways of overcoming them.** Best of all, it will inspire you to keep going when you get discouraged and want to give up.

Before you begin your journey to winning golf, you need to internalize three important ideas:

1. It's not too late for you to become a real golfer. I was a 52-year-old beginner in 1999 when I started applying the methods described in this book. **I broke 80 thirteen months into my golf career.** Despite my age, physical deficiencies and back surgery in 2001, I went from shooting in the 120s to a 3.9 handicap. **The methods described here really do work.** Age is not a factor.

2. **This book is about improving your golf *scores*, not your swing.** There's a big difference.

3. Pointless and self-limiting excuses hinder your growth as a golfer. **If you can shoot 99, you can shoot 79.** Stay focused on why you can and will get better. Golf is a ruthless teacher and

doesn't tolerate defeatist attitudes. There's always a new and brighter day ahead. You have to learn to laugh off yesterday's mistakes and keep moving toward your objective.

The methods described here require neither a swing remake nor hours a day of work. They challenge conventional methods of teaching golf. You'll find no lengthy chapters on swing hypotheses, x-factors or bio-mechanics. Such lofty ideas, factual as they might be, often serve only to baffle higher handicap golfers. Better to learn to play golf first and allow the swing to develop along the way. That's what this book is about – learning to play better golf and lowering your scores now, using the swing you have today.

Put aside those fuzzy and intimidating thoughts that equate golf success with hard labor, pain and suffering. These ideas are false. Golf improvement is simple to understand. It requires that you recognize and attack the *specific* faults that are causing you to pile up unnecessary strokes. The inability to hit a beautiful, soaring 4-iron is not what's trashing your scorecard.

I hope you have a target score you'd someday like to shoot. I hope you dream of beating golfers who have trounced you in the past. These ambitions will serve to keep you motivated during temporary setbacks. Finally, I trust you'd like to get your handicap into single digits. That skill level is a worthy goal for every motivated middle and high handi-capper and is the mark of a true golfer.

I can't promise you'll win the championship of your club or be the best player at your course, but you don't have to wait five or ten more years to finally break 80, either. Perhaps you will in the next season or two. It's certainly possible.

Get ready for some exciting and memorable times. You'll find inside no magic, no promise of 400-yard drives later this week and no silly guarantee of shooting under par in a month or two. You'll discover instead a common-sense and workable approach to lowering your golf scores in a reasonably short period of time.

If you play to a 30 handicap today, you'll still be there next week, next month, and for the rest of your life if you spend all your time trying to get "the swing" down. Swing training is one of many factors, but it's probably not what most struggling golfers need first.

When I began playing, I took a few swing lessons, but I didn't adopt the "work on the swing until you drop" routine I saw other golfers pursuing. My aching back prevented me from spending hours on the range and I was forced to choose a different practice method. I happily realized that I had chosen the correct path because I soon bypassed most of the struggling "swing masters."

There is a nearly universal – and false – belief among high-handicap golfers that you have to work hours a day to get good at this game. I have been accused of this many times, but I didn't do it. The truth is that I played often and practiced only moderately, but always intelligently and with a purpose. I firmly believe that any golfer willing to spend as little as five hours a month in productive practice can, in a season or two, progress beyond his or her wildest dreams.

Improvement won't come in steady, straight lines, but rather in fits and starts, with misfortune, frustration and backsliding always in the mix. That's the nature of golf. But improvement comes. It comes in leaps and bounds when you practice – not hard and long, but sensibly and with a purpose.

I confess: I am neither a golf pro nor a swing trainer. I write with the authority of experience – the lonely experience of a pitiful hacker who struggled against steep odds and rapidly became a real golfer. If you are skeptical of a book by a non-pro, take heart. Three golf professionals examined and wholly approved the manuscript of this book before it went to the printer.

Apply the principles in this book, and one day before long, you'll wonder why in the world you ever were happy breaking 100 or 90. You'll want to kick yourself when you shoot some really dreadful score – like 85. Becoming an eight or nine-handicapper is a realistic goal, even for golfers whose schedules limit time for practice and play.

Read through the book and reflect on the ideas presented. Honestly evaluate your own game, plan your progress, then do it! If you ever want to be a real golfer, this book is going to show you how.

The methods are enjoyable and rewarding, and they absolutely work. They'll cost you nothing more than a few tune-ups from your local golf pro, an update to your equipment, and the purchase of some proven training tools. The reward for your efforts will be extraordinary.

Despite fantastic equipment, beautifully manicured golf courses and millions of swing lessons, the average golf handicap never seems to improve. Perhaps now is a good time for high-handicap golfers to try a different approach.

Read on, resolve to make the start and stay positive. The results are certain to surprise and delight you.

Acknowledgements

First and foremost, I want to thank and acknowledge my wife, Susan. She patiently (as always) endured while I endlessly labored at my computer creating this book. I love and thank you for your kindness, honey. You're the best.

Special thanks to golf professionals Dennis Bowman, Bob Love and Scott Shepherd, who examined the manuscript and confirmed all of what I believe about how average golfers become real golfers.

Many thanks to artist David Hendren for his original illustrations.

I could never have finished this project without the editing and proofreading assistance of Margot Dokken, Alan Himber, Mary Bonds, Rebecca A. Williamson, and Bluefish Bay Editing and Publishing Services. My gratitude to one and all.

Finally, I am indebted to Pamela Trush (www.delaney-designs.com) for her creative cover design.

A couple of hours of practice is worth ten sloppy rounds. – Babe Didrikson Zaharias

PART I

HOW GOLF HAPPENED TO ME

(All references to left and right in this book assume a right-handed golfer.)

I started playing golf in the summer of 1999. In the beginning, I could barely get a ball off the ground, even with a pitching wedge. I had a lot going against me. I was fifty-two years old, I had suffered with back problems for thirteen years and I was about fifty pounds overweight. I was also a diabetic, injecting sixty to seventy units of insulin into my body every day. I started out shooting about 50 over par.

Despite these obstacles, thirteen months later I broke 80, and in another six months my handicap index had fallen to 10.1. Not long afterward, I reached the low single-digits.

****

1999 – Beginnings

On a cold March day in 1999, an old friend of mine from Dallas, the late Zola Levitt (a Bible scholar and prophecy teacher you may have watched on TV) stopped by my home near Tahlequah, Oklahoma. He revealed excitedly that he had a new hobby – golf. The man was sixty years old and was as animated as a child with a new toy. He had his new golf clubs with him and was anxious to get to a driving range.

We drove to Cherry Springs, a local golf course, and I watched him hit some practice balls. After a while, he handed me his driver and suggested I take a swing or two. I hesitated at first, citing my bad back, but as the old saying goes, I can resist "anything but temptation," and I quickly gave in. After several tries, I managed to get a couple of drives to the middle of the range. Although it felt good, I didn't return to the course until three months later, when Zola was passing through town again. It was June, and the weather was comfortable and warm. This time, he wanted me to play nine holes.

Off we went with one bag of clubs between us. As could be expected of two beginners, we hacked the course to pieces. I hobbled home with a 71 and lost by a stroke. Even though every shot I hit without a tee was a grounder, the golf bug began to nibble at my psyche.

With borrowed clubs, I was soon shooting in the 60s on nine holes, or what would calculate to a 50 handicap. But I wasn't troubled by my scores. Golf seemed magical to me, and in just a few rounds, I had fallen in love with this fascinating game. I made the decision to become a respectable golfer as quickly as I could. I didn't pick a handicap goal at the time because I didn't understand the handicap system.

In the following months, progress came rapidly, with the predictable setbacks and frustrations constantly dogging me. I subscribed to The Golf Channel and golf magazines. I took lessons and played as often as I could.

My teacher, Dennis Bowman, who was at that time the pro at Cherry Springs golf course in Tahlequah, emphasized the importance of the short game. I owe much of my golf success to the advice Dennis gave me that first tough year.

My handicap index soon dropped to 25, then 20, then 12, then 10, and finally into single digits, bottoming at 3.9, my lowest to date.

How Golf Happened to Me

As I look back, I believe that I could have accomplished what I did in far less time had I known what I do today. That's the knowledge I wish to impart to the readers of this book – ideas and practical plans for becoming a real (single-digit) golfer in the shortest time possible.

****

As I drove home from Cherry Springs that fateful March day in 1999, I thought back to my childhood dabbling in golf. My only playing partner in those days was a neighborhood friend, Jeff Moorman.

When I was eight or nine, my parents bought golf lessons for my older brother, Billy and me. We studied under Charlie Weisner, pro at the Muskogee (Oklahoma) Country Club. My brother didn't take to golf at all, but after two or three lessons, I wanted to play, so Jeff and I headed to the course. We played nine holes about a dozen times, and as I remember, I usually shot in the 70s. This was, of course from the front tees. I marveled at how anybody could play a full eighteen holes in under 100 strokes. Golf was so difficult.

A child under ten hardly ever makes a true par, much less a birdie, but it happened to me. The lone birdie of my childhood came on the short par three seventeenth hole at the Muskogee Country Club. It measured about 110 yards from the front tees. I pushed my drive off to the right. The ball fell short of the green and rolled down a hill next to a lake that separated the seventeenth green from the eighteenth tee box. I was left with about 25 yards up the hill, over a ridge, and onto the green. I didn't trust any club to fly the hill, so I pulled out my putter. I could see only the top of the flagstick. I slammed my putter at the ball and watched it race up the hill and disappear over the crest. All of a sudden, I heard a clanking sound, and on the green, Jeff started screaming, "You made it! You made it!" Stunned, I jumped in the air. "Birdie!" I shrieked as I fell down and rolled to the bottom of the hill. The memory of that birdie remains a highlight of my youth.

Make Your Golf Dream A Reality

Jeff's father died in an airplane crash in 1957. His mother eventually remarried and the family moved to Oklahoma City. With Jeff gone, my golf came to an abrupt halt. I discontinued lessons and my kiddie clubs disappeared forever into a closet. My interests turned to football, basketball and track.

Golf surrounded me and I should have stayed with it. My grandfather, Louis W. Duncan, was club champion at the Muskogee Country Club in 1917, 1925, 1937, and 1938. He was fifty-two the last time he won it. My father, A.G. "Bill" Hays, though never an avid golfer, played to about a 15 handicap. An injury to his shoulder in the 1960s put an end to his golf. A first cousin of mine, Jim Buchanan, was a 3-handicapper as a high school golfer and played for Harvard in the 1960s. The highlight of his college golf career was a holed chip shot on the 17th hole at The Country Club in Brookline, Massachusetts to defeat his Yale opponent 2-1. Golf fans in the United States have fond memories of that hole as well, thanks to a Justin Leonard putt in the 1999 Ryder Cup.

After Jeff moved away, more than forty years would pass before I picked up my friend's driver at the Cherry Springs range.

****

I moved back to Oklahoma in 1998 after living nineteen years in Dallas. Tahlequah is a resort/retirement/farming community of about fifteen thousand, located on Highway 62, seventy miles southeast of Tulsa.

My wife, Susan, and I live south of town on what was once a hunting and fishing club. The club was founded by a group of sportsmen from eastern Oklahoma in 1908 and is located on a pretty thirty-acre tract next to the Illinois River.

The wives and children of the club founders soon realized that they were missing out on a lot of fun, and within a few years, club members began building summer cabins. An Olympic-sized swimming pool and tennis courts were added later. A central dining room, serving three meals a day all summer, delighted the wives, and happy children trekked the grounds, riverbed, and nearby pastures on horseback. Golf carts and ATVs have replaced the horses in recent years. My family joined the club in 1948, when I was a year old.

My childhood golf pal, Jeff Moorman, is also a longtime club member. Although he still lives in Oklahoma City, he visits here most weekends in the summertime. Jeff dropped golf for a few years after he left Muskogee, but when he was about twelve or thirteen, he found a set of Henry Pickard hickory-shaft irons in the closet of his stepfather, Walter Stark. Stark had been the manager of Twin Hills Country Club years earlier and had been given the clubs by Henry Pickard himself at the end of a big tournament.

Jeff says he took the nine-iron and spent many happy hours hitting balls back and forth across the street in front of his house, pretending that the pavement was a river. He then moved to a park down the street and practiced hitting balls to trees and other make-believe holes. When Jeff got to college, he and some fraternity brothers would take wedges and play a homemade mini-course. Instead of golf holes, they used water meters, sprinkler heads, and other designated spots around the fraternity house to make up the course. Jeff told me they played this game for hours on end. He never took a swing lesson in his life, but he's always had an excellent short game and at age fifty-eight is still able to break 80 from the blue tees.

I share Jeff's story to make a salient point: a golfer with a good short game can compete against anybody. I've seen Jeff shoot in the low 70s more than once. He knows how to get a golf ball into the hole from anywhere around the green.

****

In the summer of 1998, I observed that other members of the club where I live spent many happy days playing golf. Evening meals were filled with boisterous talk and laughter recounting the day's events on the course. When Labor Day weekend came, the club sponsored its annual team golf scramble, which included prizes and a name plaque awarded to the winning team. At that point in time, I was neither a golfer nor a fisherman, so when the summer of 1999 rolled around, golf became an ideal way for me to have a good time with the crowd.

Once I showed an interest in the game, Jeff loaned me an old set of blade-style irons. I am about four inches taller than he is, and the clubs were cut too short. I eagerly drove to Cherry Springs to hit my first bucket of practice balls. The range was busy when I got there and I felt self-conscious, so I crept to the far left side where the other golfers couldn't see me.

I took out the nine-iron and made my first swing. *Clunk!* The ball rolled about 80 yards. I tried again. *Clunk!* I tried the seven-iron, made a big cut, and got the same unsettling thud.

After several more embarrassing attempts, I grabbed my clubs and practice balls, got into the car and waited for the range to clear. Forty-five minutes later, I returned and finished grounding the rest of the bucket. I returned home discouraged. Was it me or the irons, or both? I never got a ball to fly higher than my belt buckle that day.

I scheduled a lesson with the club pro, Dennis Bowman. I explained that I was a beginner and couldn't get a ball off the ground unless it was on a tee. Dennis surprised me when he asked me to take out the pitching wedge and start hitting balls to a tree about 40 yards away. He watched my short swings and corrected my setup position. With Dennis helping, I was quickly able to get these shots into the air. He advised me to keep practicing short shots. Accurate short shots, he explained, are what golf is really all about. That statement, coming from a golf professional, made a deep impression on me back then, and its significance has stayed with me ever since.

After the lesson with Dennis, I played nine holes several times with some improvement, but I was still shooting in the 55-60 range. My back hurt most of the time, and I dreaded even trying to play eighteen holes.

Natural Golf

Later in the summer an infomercial on The Golf Channel caught my attention. The ad was for Natural Golf, and it advertised a swing that was easier on the back. That's exactly what I was looking for and I ordered the information package and tapes that same night.

It arrived a few days later and was filled with good ideas. Natural Golf stressed a wider stance and a ten-finger grip, and the guys in the video were making compact swings with less body rotation. The video compared the conventional swing to the simpler Natural Golf swing. It was obvious that the Natural golfers were turning and twisting their backs far less than the conventional golfers. Natural Golf may not be for everybody, but it was perfect for my situation.

My packet advertised an upcoming Natural Golf class to be held in Dallas, four hours away, and I immediately enrolled. The class was taught at Sleepy Hollow Country Club, about twenty minutes south of downtown Dallas, just off Interstate 45. Sleepy Hollow is a quaint, old-style country club with two eighteen-hole courses, the Lake and River.

I dutifully arrived with Jeff's short clubs in hand and found about fifteen other students signed up for the course. Our instructor, Billy Golden, introduced himself and discussed the Natural Golf system with us for an hour or so. Afterwards we proceeded to the range. As we began hitting balls, Billy noticed my ill-fitting equipment and handed me a Natural Golf nine-iron.

Using the setup and ten-finger grip Billy had shown us, I lined up and made a swing. The ball sailed high and straight about 130 yards! It was the best iron shot of my life. I was fascinated and continued hitting balls with this magic nine-iron. The difference between this modern golf club and those in my borrowed set was astonishing.

Billy worked with the group all morning and allowed me to hit many of the Natural Golf irons. The longer irons were more difficult to hit, but they were still far superior to those in my old set. I learned an important lesson that day: the easiest way to improve your golf game is to get better equipment.

At the end of the Natural Golf class, I sat down with Billy and ordered a full set of Natural Golf irons along with a driver, three wood, and seven wood. I had to wait a couple of weeks for my new clubs to arrive, but a wonderful accident happened. When I returned to Oklahoma and took my clubs out of the car, I noticed that the Natural Golf nine-iron was still in my bag. Joy!

I let Billy Golden know what had happened and got an address to send the nine-iron back – but asked if I could keep it until my new set arrived. Billy graciously let me keep the magic club for the next two weeks. Because it was the only club that I could really hit, I used it everywhere. I would hit a wood off the tee and nine-irons the rest of the way to the hole, even on the par fives. On par threes, I would often drive with the nine-iron, pitch with the nine-iron, and chip with the nine-iron. I found that any club you can reliably hit straight 125–130 yards is a great asset, particularly to a golfer who's used to hacking his way around the course in 120 strokes.

At the Natural Golf school, I had learned about aiming, setting up with a wider stance, the ten-finger grip and making a more compact swing. We also took sand and chipping lessons. Even with all this education, I still hadn't broken 100 by the time my new clubs finally arrived in early September.

I took a couple of more lessons from Dennis, and following his advice, I began to spend thirty minutes to an hour every week practicing chipping and short pitches. I often played alone and I began to analyze each round. Although every aspect of my game was terrible, the most frustrating part was finding myself within 40 yards of the green and needing four or five more shots to get the ball in the hole.

My long game was good enough to get me to within 100 yards of many greens in regulation (one shot on a par three, two on a par four, and three on a par five), but I simply could not put the ball anywhere close to the hole from short distances. In fact, most of the time, I couldn't even get it onto the green. Double and triple bogeys filled my scorecards.

By now, I had spent many evenings watching The Golf Channel. I saw the great players scramble for birdie and par from everywhere. The wide variety of shots the tour pros could play was amazing to me. It was dawning on me that if I was ever going to be a golfer, I would have to learn how to put a ball on the green from 100 yards and closer.

How Golf Happened to Me

I played plenty of golf and continued to review the basics I had learned at golf school. When one problem became worse than the others I was experiencing, I would see Dennis and work out the immediate difficulty. I learned that an occasional tune-up by a professional was the best money I could spend. In five minutes, Dennis could analyze and correct an error that I might never discover and fix on my own. As with most high handicappers, my troubles were almost always caused by faulty setup and aim.

In late August, I lost an eighteen-hole round against Dr. Charles Fullenwider, a good friend and retired Muskogee physician. I don't remember the exact scores, but between the two of us, we hit at least 250 shots. I just happened to hit a few more than Charles did. My problem the whole day was that suddenly and inexplicably, I couldn't get a tee shot into the air and I had no inkling why. Charlie and I planned a repeat match for the following week, so I had to do something about my tee shots.

I visited Cherokee Trails Golf Club in Tahlequah a few days later, and ran into the pro, Mike Palmer. I mentioned my troubles with the driver and Mike handed me a bucket of balls and sent me out to warm up. On the range, he watched me hit a few grounders. "Drop your right shoulder two inches," he told me, "and stay behind the ball." I didn't know what he meant by staying behind the ball, but I set up my usual way, dropped my right shoulder two inches and made a swing.

Crack!

The ball sailed high in the air about 230 yards, right on the line I had picked. I couldn't believe my eyes. With my right shoulder dropped, I hit shot after shot this way, woods and irons alike, with vast improvement in the quality of hits. This setup correction caused a transformation in my game. Armed with my new ball-striking skill, I knocked several strokes off of my score and soundly beat Charlie a few days later.

September came, and I began practicing at the Cherry Springs putting green for fifteen to twenty minutes at a time, putting the nine holes and trying to break "par" of eighteen shots. Then I would hit fifteen or twenty chip shots. Although I didn't realize it at the time, these short sessions would soon pay off.

For variety, I began playing different courses within an hour's drive of home. On September 21, 1999, I achieved the first major goal of my golf career. I drove the half-hour to Sequoyah State Park Golf Course at Western Hills in Hulbert, Oklahoma. Sequoyah Park is a pretty, state-managed course that runs along the banks of Fort Gibson Lake. It's short and hilly, measuring only 5,860 yards from the men's tees, but dense woods, rocky terrain and water come into play on practically every hole.

I was playing well by my standards, shooting 50 on the front nine. After fourteen holes, I noticed that I was going to be pressed to keep an appointment with my dentist in Muskogee, twenty miles away. A quick check of the scorecard revealed that I still had a chance to break 100. This would be my first time, and I wasn't about to quit early. It was a Tuesday afternoon and the course was nearly empty, so I was able to get through the final four holes in record time. As I stepped onto the eighteenth tee box, I knew all I needed was a bogey five to shoot 99.

Eighteen measures only 340 yards, but it plays uphill with thick woods on the right. I managed to keep my drive in the fairway, but left my second shot about ten yards short of the green. Down in three, and I break 100! The green sits like a table on top of a steep hill. I needed to land the ball below the pin to avoid a downhill putt, but I feared that anything hit short could roll back and end up behind me. My heart was racing. I didn't know when I'd get another chance like this one. I pulled out my sand wedge and somehow managed to stop the ball on the green fifteen feet from the hole. Two putts cemented my beautiful 99. It was a joyful drive to the dentist's office.

It's easier to keep breaking 100 once you've proved you can do it. Ten days later I shot another 99 at Sequoyah, and two days after that I shot 95 at the more difficult Cherry Springs course, followed by a 98 a week later. The fun was beginning.

I traveled to Connecticut, New Hampshire, and Maine in mid-October and played several beautiful golf courses, but I wasn't able to break 100. Back home at Cherry Springs on the twenty-third of that month, I shot what was the round of a lifetime to that point. I hit the ball well and made several nice chips and one-putt par saves to get home in 85 strokes. A few short hours of chipping and putting practice had paid a nice dividend.

Around this time, I discovered several high-quality golf books. I bought *Dave Pelz's Short Game Bible* and Dr. Bob Rotella's *Golf Is Not a Game of Perfect* and *Golf Is a Game of Confidence*. These books, along with David Leadbetter's *Faults and Fixes—How to Correct the 80 Most Common Problems in Golf*, I still consider the most valuable in my library.

Dr. Rotella is a sports psychologist from Virginia. His books have helped a wide range of golfers, from PGA tour pro down to the beginner, learn how to think their way through 18 holes of golf. The stories of improving amateurs in Rotella's books were inspiring to me and I wanted to know how these amateurs had become better golfers. Pelz's *Short Game Bible* was so long and detailed, it overwhelmed me. I glanced through it quickly and decided to set it aside for a while. Big mistake.

The final few weeks of 1999 found me breaking 100 most of the time, and even 90 on rare occasions. By now, the golf bug had bitten deeply into me, and I entered 2000 with high hopes for sustained progress.

2000 – A Short Game Education

As the year 2000 began, I was hard focused on moving up another level. My goal for the year was to break 90 on a regular basis, and I was fortunate to be able to achieve this.

I continued to analyze every round and always came to the same conclusion: short game mistakes were killing my scores. I occasionally got up and down from off the green, but I still had way too many "down in four or five" holes to have a chance to break 80.

I got Pelz's *Short Game Bible* back out and began what I at first imagined would be a long and grueling task. Wrong again.

My handicap had dropped to the low 20s during the first two months of 2000. That spring, I joined the Muskogee Country Club (MCC). Even though the club is a twenty-five-mile drive from my home, the quality of the course and practice facilities made it a bargain.

Make Your Golf Dream A Reality

Muskogee Country Club is one of the finest courses in the state, designed by Perry Maxwell, creator of the famous Southern Hills Country Club in Tulsa and many other excellent courses around the U.S. At 6,320 yards from men's tees, MCC is not long, but this course is tough! Everybody scoffs at the official USGA course rating of 70.2 and slope of 125 – it's harder than that. The fairways are narrow and trees come into play on every hole. The greens are slick and undulating. Land a ball on the wrong side of one of these hilly monsters, and three-putts are as likely as two. Garage-size bunkers surround most holes. Although the course is beautifully manicured and loads of fun to play, it is still like a visit to boot camp. The club pro once told me that if I could learn to score well at MCC, other courses would seem easy.

One reason I joined MCC was to take advantage of the excellent short game practice area. It's 115 yards long with a huge green and two large practice bunkers. Around the back of the green are rolling hills, just like on the course and I could easily practice from either fairway or rough. Markers at 50 and 100 yards made it simple to step off precise yardages for distance control practice with the wedges.

My study of Pelz's *Short Game Bible* was going pretty slowly. Pelz, a former NASA engineer, is brilliant, but analytical to a fault. In the first eighty pages of the book he explains the importance of the short game, concepts of the short game, the five different games of golf, mechanics of the short game, stances, ball positions, finesse swing planes, body turns – all in minute detail. He even has a chart showing how much money he lost in his first few years in the golf business.

One concept that stayed with me is found on Pelz's putting conversion chart. I was shocked to learn that the distance at which the best professional golfers miss half their putts is only six feet. Pelz touts what he calls the "Golden Eight" theory. He explains that if you can hit your approach or chip shots to within eight feet of the hole, you have a real chance of one-putting and saving a full stroke. Anything outside of eight feet, whether it's twelve or forty feet, will most likely result in a two-putt.

How Golf Happened to Me

If a golfer can learn to control distance inside 100 yards of the green and start getting the ball into Pelz's "Golden Eight," that golfer's handicap will drop like a rock.

I didn't know it at the time, but when I got to page 81, Chapter 5, *How to Score*, my golf game was about to make a huge leap for the better. Pelz explains his 3x4 system of wedge play, three swings for four wedges, producing exact distances (see Chapter 7 of this book, *Distance Control, The Secret of Golf*, for an explanation of these finesse swings).

I couldn't wait to try out this system. At the time, I had only a pitching wedge and sand wedge, so I bought a 60-degree lob wedge and started working on a 3x3 system (three finesse swings for each of three wedges).

I spent about half an hour at home practicing the finesse swing described by Pelz. Next, I went to the range, got my pitching wedge, and went to the 50-yard marker. I practiced a few 7:30 swings (hands go back to 7:30 position on an imaginary clock with your head representing 12:00 and the ball 6:00), set up an aim club and started hitting balls. (See Figure 5, page 83 of this book). It was awkward at first and I quickly noticed that most shots were going past the flag. I backed up 5 yards and hit another batch of balls. This proved to be the correct distance for the 7:30 pitching wedge swing, so I wrote down 55 yards. Even with the many mis-hits figured in, this took only about twenty minutes.

Next, I backed up to 75 yards and repeated the test with a 9:00 swing (hands back to 9:00 on the imaginary clock). Twenty minutes and many mis-hits later, I had learned that 80 yards was the correct distance for this swing. I then backed up to 100 yards and started making 10:30 swings. Again, a little feedback revealed that 105 yards was the distance produced by this swing. I got a strip of paper and wrote down 55, 80, and 105 and taped it to the shaft of the pitching wedge. I had just acquired three new shots.

Later in the week, I went through the same process with my sand and lob wedges. Following Pelz's recommendations, I wrote down the three distances produced for each wedge on strips of paper, cut them out, and taped them to the shafts of these wedges.

The entire process was easy and I completed it in less than one week. After that, for the next couple of months, whenever I went to the golf course I would spend twenty or thirty minutes at the short game range, practicing my new wedge shots.

It felt as if I had put a half dozen new clubs in my bag when I learned to control distance with my new wedge swings. Now when I was 55 yards from the green, I could hit a 7:30 pitching wedge and have some chance of getting it to within eight or ten feet of the flag. By adding or subtracting a little from known swings, I could hit the ball close from any short distance. A shot of 45 yards would be a 7:30 sand wedge; 85 yards, a 9:15 pitching wedge; and 65 yards, slightly less than a 9:00 sand wedge. When I could execute the correct swing, it worked like magic. Naturally, I still made many mis-hits, but at least I wasn't guessing at how to hit these shots any more. I knew what shot was supposed to produce a certain distance, and a poor result was caused by faulty execution, not bad planning or guessing. A wonderful side benefit of this practice was that I began to sense the feel of swinging smoothly and rhythmically.

I began practicing my distance wedge shots early in 2000. With my new short game weapons, my handicap dropped fast. I started the year with close to a 22 handicap. Soon it was down to 18. By the middle of June, it was 15.5; in September, after bouncing around in the mid to low teens all summer, at one point it reached a low for the year of 11.8. My long game and putting had not noticeably changed during this period. I attribute my drop in handicap directly to my new ability to hit more accurate shots from inside 100 yards, thereby saving a full stroke four to eight times per round. Double bogeys turned into bogeys. Bogeys became pars. I had discovered the secret of golf – distance control.

The cooler and more difficult winter golf weather led to a handicap increase back to 13.9 by year's end, but this was still a great result for one season. A good number of my rounds in 2000 were played at the difficult Muskogee Country Club course, further proving the immense value of my short game and wedge practice.

How Golf Happened to Me

From my own experience, I can confidently predict that any high-handicap golfer who employs three or four wedges and spends a few hours learning measured swings and precise distances can drop his or her handicap six to ten strokes in one season. It doesn't take "hours a day" or even hours a week. A high-handicap golfer willing to spend just a few productive hours per month acquiring and maintaining proficiency at these shots will reap a marvelous and quick payoff. That's not a lot to ask.

I continued playing often, always evaluating my rounds in terms of fairways, greens in regulation, and putting. In the fall of the year 2000, I had my first experience with the yips. This nervous condition is defined by difficulty in holing short putts, and is brought on by recent failures to do just that. Ben Hogan fought the yips and even suggested that putts should count only as a half-stroke. Sam Snead changed his style of putting several times to escape the yips. Johnny Miller claims he started yipping at age nineteen.

Other well-known golfers have successfully battled their putting woes with innovative grip changes. Chris DiMarco and Mark O'Meara come to mind, with their respective "claw" and "saw" grips. The long putter, another anti-yip weapon, has an excellent history, especially on the European tour. Sam Torrance, Mark James, Bernhard Langer, and CBS golf commentator David Feherety have all favored the long putter at one time or another.

I had begun missing a lot of putts of three and four feet. This caused me to become anxious about short putts, which made me keep missing. Pretty soon I was more fearful of a short putt than of a heart attack. I dug through my golf books and consulted a professional, looking for answers.

I eventually settled on two very simple, but effective, remedies. The first one was scary. On any putt of less than five feet, I would get set up, line up the putter, start the backswing, then close my eyes as the putter started forward. After stroking the ball, I would wait long enough to hear it drop into the cup.

It was very hard not to look, and I admit this method took some getting used to, but it worked well. Initially, I had a fear of not striking the ball solidly or scraping the putter against the green, but that didn't happen. With my eyes closed, I had no way to watch the ball, so there was no reason to jerk the club or to move my head. My first case of yips was cured almost immediately, and I was soon confidently putting with my regular style. By the way, nobody seems to notice when you putt with your eyes closed. They're watching the ball.

Putting tips and fixes all seem to communicate one important message: Don't move *anything* but the arms and shoulders until well after the ball has left the putter face. On short putts, don't ever watch the ball. With eyes closed or open, make the stroke, keep your head perfectly still and listen for the ball to rattle into the cup.

A couple of years after my first case of the yips, I was playing at Cherry Springs with my cousin, Jim Buchanan, and some old Muskogee friends, Bob and Sarah Voegeli. Though I can't say I was yipping, I did miss two or three short putts on the front nine. Finally, on the fourteenth hole, I missed another four-footer. Bob Voegeli gave me a suggestion that immediately set me straight. To stop peeking, he said, set up normally, get the putter aimed precisely down your target line, then stare at the hole and stroke it in. The theory is that you don't have to move your head or body to see if you make it. You're already "peeking" before you even start the stroke. This method also focuses your brain on the target. I began making almost all of my short putts after this tip.

If short putts start troubling you, try either of these methods. Spend fifteen or twenty minutes practicing the new method before you take it to the course. It will feel very different from conventional putting. That is what you want, though, a complete departure from the troubling pattern of missed short putts. Once you get used to your short putts banging into the back of the cup, your confidence will return and your short putt troubles will be over, at least for a while.

These remedies are effective for putts of five feet and shorter. Maintain your normal putting style for longer putts, keeping everything but your arms and shoulders perfectly still.

Despite the previously mentioned setbacks in the late autumn, 2000 was a very successful year, with many important lessons learned and a handicap drop of eight strokes.

2001 –Toughing It Out

In December of 2000, the Muskogee Country Club closed for nine months to recondition the greens. I returned to the Cherry Springs and Tahlequah City courses locally and to Cobblestone Creek and Eagle Crest in Muskogee until September of 2001.

The year 2001 proved to be the most challenging of my early golf career. I began the year with a 13.9 handicap and finished at 10.5. That spring I had come close to getting my handicap index into single digits, dropping at one point to 10.1.

During the last week of June, I met two friends to play Eagle Crest Golf Course in Muskogee. As I warmed up at the range, my back began to ache on the lower left side. This happened all the time, so I ignored it. It hurt more and more as the day wore on, and by the time we finished, I wasn't playing golf, I was just trying to stay vertical.

I hobbled home and scheduled an appointment with my friend, Muskogee neurosurgeon Dr. Chuck Fullenwider, son of the previously mentioned Charles. The office visit and MRI indicated disk problems, and surgery was scheduled for July 11.

I first injured my back in a 1986 tennis match. Although I was in pain much of the time, I spent the next fifteen years trying to avoid surgery. Throughout these years, I constantly had the feeling that the left side of my neck and my left heel were being pulled together by a giant rubber band, and I had to keep stretching and pulling them apart in order to relieve the stiffness and pain. I went to orthopedic doctors and chiropractors, took physical therapy, and learned numerous back exercises to help alleviate the pain. These actions delayed the inevitable, but the pain and imbalance following the round at Eagle Crest was the worst that I had ever experienced.

When I woke up in the hospital a few hours after my surgery, the pulling sensation in my back was gone. For the first time in fifteen years, my left leg felt as if it was attached normally. I spent the next two months slowly recuperating and missing golf terribly.

After Labor Day I was able to begin chipping and putting, and on September 26, eleven weeks after my surgery, I played my first eighteen-hole round, carding an 81 at the Muskogee Country Club.

Dr. Fullenwider told me that my handicap would probably get better after the operation. He maintains that most golfers improve following back surgery because they slow down and swing more smoothly. Since my surgery, I make my full swings at eighty percent of full power, as Natural Golf's Moe Norman always taught. I still get enough distance, but better accuracy.

As I recuperated, my golf was spotty. Susan and I went to Florida for about ten days after Christmas and I got to play a number of entertaining rounds at The Villages, an amazing golf resort near Lady Lake, Florida. My friend Zola Levitt and his wife, Sandra, had rented a house for the winter months and invited us down for a visit.

Everyone who lives in The Villages is retirement age, and these people love to play golf. In addition to standard streets, The Villages has built golf cart paths to every place imaginable. You can visit the doctor, hospital, supermarket, convenience store, discount store, restaurant, theater, or shopping mall in your golf cart. Drive around town, and you see golf carts (with clubs loaded and ready) in almost every garage. It's as close to a golfer's paradise as I have ever seen.

Despite my medical setbacks, the year 2001 could be considered a success. Even with the surgery, my handicap had dropped to 10.5. I remained on the edge of single-digit handicap status.

2002 – A Year of Milestones

2002 was a better year, and by April, I had recovered most of the strength I lost from the back operation.

I achieved three major milestones in 2002. First, on February 28, I finally broke into single-digits. My handicap fell to 9.9 following the round at the Muskogee Country Club that day. Second, I made an official hole-in-one. On March 24, I went to MCC to practice and play nine holes. After a few minutes of hitting distance wedges and sand shots, I went to the range. It was a happy golf day. My rhythm was just right, and I was hitting the ball right on the screws. The round started well, and I was one under par after four holes. I finished the front nine at one over par (37) and stopped by the pro shop to look for a playing partner for the back nine. I didn't want to quit on a day like this. I was lucky and was able to join a threesome, including the club pro's father, on their way to the tenth tee.

When we got to the par-three twelfth hole, I took out my five-iron, teed the ball up, and got ready to hit. Just before starting my backswing, I felt uncomfortable looking at the ball. To this day I don't know why, but I leaned down and re-teed the ball about two inches to the right of its original spot. Then, I set up and made my swing.

The ball flew as straight as an arrow toward the flagstick, bounced once on the front of the green and rolled right into the hole!

That round was magical, as I achieved my all-time low score (to that point in time) of 75 at MCC, marred by a double-bogey on the eighteenth hole. Eight months later, on a cold November day, while playing alone from the tips, I made another ace on the same hole with a seven-wood from 185 yards. Unofficial.

I achieved my third milestone on June 19, 2002, when I shot a 1-under-par round of 67 (with five birdies) at the short par 68 Tahlequah City golf course. This was my first time to shoot under par and to break 70. There wasn't much wind that day, and I was lucky to sink several putts longer than ten feet. I'd have to wait over two years to do it again. In October of 2004, I managed a smooth 68 at the forgiving par-70 Lake Park course near Dallas with two birdies in the last four holes.

My practice routine remained the same during this period. I tried to spend twenty to thirty minutes once or twice a week working on my distance wedge shots and verifying distances. Wedge shot distances change slightly in varying temperatures, so every season is different. I tried to hit at least fifteen sand shots, chips, and short pitches at these practice sessions. I would hit thirty or forty balls on the range before playing, using an aim club and picking a target for every shot. Then, I would spend five to ten minutes on the practice green right before playing. The last couple of minutes before teeing off I spent holing putts of three and four feet.

The reader can see that my routine required a relatively small investment of time and effort. Any serious golfer has the time to utilize such a routine. To rapidly improve your golf, it's essential to spend these few hours each month on this simple training.

I played pretty well the whole season and my handicap index dropped as low as 6.8 at one point. I finished at 7.4, a drop of over three points. It was a good year, and I gained much valuable experience.

2002 left me with many pleasant memories.

2003 – A Real Golfer

In January, I started playing more golf than ever before. I could now comfortably play with the "big boys" and flat bellies. I began shooting in the 70s about half the time, and often in the low 70s. I shot above 90 only once in 2003.

I was good enough to play at least a credible game of golf with anybody. It was during one of my better runs that year that my handicap index dropped to an all-time best of 3.9.

In late June, I played in the Oklahoma State Senior Championship, for players fifty years of age and older with handicaps under 8.0. The tournament was played at Muskogee Country Club. I began a tournament pattern at this tournament – alternating good and bad rounds.

As I remember, there were about fifty-five players in this stroke play event. Everyone played two rounds, and the top twenty and ties played a third round to decide the champion. My drive on the first hole rolled against a tree trunk, and that was a hint of things to come. Just about everything that could go wrong went wrong that day, and I finished with a disappointing 86. Day two, I shot a more respectable 79.

My next tournament was the MCC Club Championship, senior division, a thirty-six-hole stroke play event played in August. This time, my first round was the good one. I shot 74 and was only one stroke off the lead. Another sickening 86 followed the next day, capped by a triple-bogey seven on the difficult eighteenth hole.

In October, I played in the "Best Player in the County" tournament at Cherry Springs. This tournament was limited to players thirty and older, which limited my chances. I was now fifty-six years old.

The bad round came first this time. The tournament was played from the championship tees, some 6,814 yards. This was 500 yards longer than the courses I was accustomed to playing. Something about the number 86 must have been in my mind in these tournaments, because I managed to shoot that number once again in the first round.

Nobody had been hot that first day, and the leader shot 77 or 78. Day two was time for my good round again, and my ball-striking and short game both showed up. I finished with a 77, five or six shots behind my friend Bob Batson, the eventual winner.

2003 ended with another trip to Florida. My friend Zola and his wife, Sandra, had bought an RV and were camped in Clermont at a park with an eighteen-hole golf course. One morning, as we waited to tee off at the Clerbrook golf course, we had the good fortune to run into a semi-retired golf teacher from Arkansas named Bob Love. Love has wintered in the Clermont area for decades and was familiar with every course in the area. We played several interesting rounds with Bob during our weeklong visit and received some first-rate instruction. He has remained a good friend and valuable coach over the years. You'll find examples of his teaching later in the book.

The year 2003 was a happy time for me. My handicap was in the mid-to-low single digits and I had become a real golfer.

Although my own golf progress was significantly slowed by an initial lack of knowledge and back surgery, I believe that any motivated golfer who earnestly practices the principles taught in this book can accomplish what I did in two or three seasons.

As I approach my sixtieth birthday, I continue to play and enjoy this beautiful game. I still play 6,300-yard and longer courses and shoot in the 70s more often than not. I continue to monitor and work on faults as they show up in my own game. It's a never-ending process, not only for the high-handicapper, but for every serious golfer, right up to the PGA tour pro.

****

The remaining chapters are devoted to coaching you to a single-digit handicap or whatever your golf goal might be. The reward for just a few hours of intelligent practice each month is magnificent, so keep your attention on where you're going and don't get down on yourself over a disappointing round or two.

Follow the guidelines and practice regularly, but don't overdo it. Five hours each month spent working on your weaknesses (and not only on what you enjoy practicing) is plenty.

Keep in mind that in golf you can't be perfect. You need to play from the right tees, learn to make better misses, be certain you're setting up and aiming straight, develop a few reliable distance control shots, and play conservatively enough to minimize blowup holes.

Stay positive and get started. You can do this.

PART II

HOW TO BECOME
A REAL GOLFER

1

Set Your Goal

Most high handicap golfers play year after year without getting any better. Some don't care – they just enjoy being outdoors and getting the exercise. Others would like to improve, but they are unwilling to make a commitment and risk failure. Still others truly desire to get into single digits, but don't know how. Another group simply has the "I can't" sign hanging in front of their eyes.

What is your personal goal as a golfer? How long have you been stuck at your current level? Who would you like to be able to beat? Get ready for some fun. You're going to learn how to reach your golf goals with the efficient and effective methods you'll discover here.

I can tell you from personal experience that watching your handicap fall and effortlessly beating players who once seemed invincible are terrific rewards for the modest effort required to reach that point.

Make Your Golf Dream A Reality

Decide what you want and be reasonable about it. If you are a 30-handicapper, you probably won't be at scratch in one season, but your game can be greatly improved. Pick your goal and commit to following through regardless of the roadblocks you have to overcome. A solid commitment means you're operating under the belief that you will reach your goal and you aren't quitting until you attain it. Make such a commitment and you're halfway there.

You'll need this dedication when times get tough. Golf is not for the fainthearted. Frustration and humiliation will be regular companions on your road to improvement. You're going to have to learn to brush it off and keep coming back. Bad things happen, even to the best of golfers. If you don't believe me, observe the fortunes of tour players on any Sunday afternoon.

Fortunately, extraordinary things happen, too. Happy golf days will come when you least expect them. You can't predict when you'll make an eagle, hole a sand shot to win a match, or shoot your all-time best round. These thrilling experiences are what make golf so unpredictable and fun.

It's easy to keep track of your handicap online or through your local golf course. I've used the Yahoo.com golf handicap tracker for several years. You'll find more on handicap trackers later in the book.

It's a good idea to keep track of your statistics in order to pinpoint weaknesses. After every round, add up the number of fairways and greens you hit. Then count your putts. Seven or eight-handicappers will hit six to nine fairways and five to ten greens in an eighteen-hole round. They will putt somewhere between twenty-eight and thirty-four times. These numbers would result in scores in the 78 to 83 range. This skill level is within reach of the truly motivated golfer who works *smart*. What's important for these golfers to notice after every round is why they were over par and what mistakes caused the extra strokes.

If they hit only four greens, how many times did they fail to get up and down for par? Maybe they hit so few greens because they missed

Set Your Goal

too many fairways and spent the day scrambling. Were there more putts than usual? Only after such analysis can a thinking golfer take logical steps to overcome faults that are spoiling the scorecard.

POINTS TO REMEMBER

- Set a handicap goal.
- Track your handicap online.
- Keep track of your statistics so you can take the correct steps to reach your goal.
- Stay with it when the going gets tough.

2

Saving Strokes

Before you can start trimming strokes from your score, you have to identify where they are coming from. Honestly analyze your game and you will quickly learn why you're not shooting in the 70s today.

Look at it this way: a perfectly played eighteen-hole "par" round of golf on a regulation course could be recorded as follows:

Tee shots = 18 strokes
Fairway shots (getting your ball onto the green) = 18 strokes
Two putts per green = 36 strokes
Total = 72 strokes

It's obvious from these numbers that you have three jobs: (1) hit a decent tee shot, (2) get your ball onto the green, and (3) putt the ball into the hole. To shoot a round of even-par 72, you must, according to this formula, hit eighteen drives, spend eighteen more shots getting your ball on the green, and putt thirty-six times.

Of course it doesn't work that way. Weekend golfers do hit eighteen drives and might well hit only thirty-six putts, but instead of shooting 72, they will score 95 to 120. Where did all the extra strokes come from? Struggling to put the ball onto the green after the tee shot, and that's where weak golfers can rapidly learn to save a bundle of strokes.

95-shooters are not accurate enough to hit many greens in regulation. The shot that is supposed to put them on the green usually only gets them somewhere within 100 yards of the flagstick, particularly if the tee shot was less than ideal. If they hit the green on the next shot and two-putt, they score bogey, or what translates to 90 on the scorecard. Sometimes, they take two or more strokes to get on the green from 100 yards and still two-putt. If that happens very often, they're on the way to shooting well over 100.

Becoming a good enough ball striker to hit nine or ten greens in regulation takes some effort, even if you're playing from tees suited to your length. Many tour pros hit only twelve to fourteen greens per round. It is far easier and quicker to learn to hit 100-yard (and shorter) shots to the green and one-putt, or to pitch over a bunker and one-putt, or chip close to the hole and one-putt. Good short shots save strokes and the payoff is immediate – a good putt, pitch, or chip usually saves a full stroke. Every golfer has the strength to execute these shots, and they appear to be easy – so people don't spend time practicing them. Everybody loves hitting long drives down the center of the fairway, but making par after par from off the green is gratifying, too.

If a 95-shooter, who in eighteen holes might hit only two or three greens in regulation, could chip or pitch close enough to the hole to one-putt five to eight times per round, that golfer would immediately be shooting in the eighties without changing anything else. The ability to become skilled at this is a hundred times easier than learning to draw a four-iron around a tree and onto a distant green.

Unless you're already a good short game player (in which case you don't shoot 95), you will learn in this book how to lower your handicap by five to ten shots in a brief time, and how to become a real golfer in two or three seasons.

As an improving golfer, your long game needs to be good enough to keep you in play and get near most greens in regulation figures. When your approach shots miss the green, you're left with a short wedge shot, pitch, or chip onto the green in one over regulation figures (on the green in 3 strokes on a par 4, etc.). As soon as you learn some distance control shots with the wedges, you'll start making many nice one-putt pars. With skillful use of the wedges, you'll take double-bogey or worse out of play most of the time, shoot lower scores, and rapidly become a happy golfer.

POINTS TO REMEMBER

- High handicappers waste numerous shots getting onto the green.
- A good short shot saves a full stroke.
- Every golfer has enough strength to make short shots.
- High handicappers can quickly reduce their scores by five to eight shots by learning to control distance with the wedges.

3

Update Your Equipment

Most readers of this book probably have modern equipment and don't need to read this chapter, but if you're a new golfer, or if you haven't played for a few years, you're about to experience an eye-opening revelation. Updating your equipment is an easy way to put new life into your golf game. Modern gear costs a little money, but it's worth it. If you truly want to be your best at golf, getting the right equipment is essential.

The right clubs, shafts, and ball exist for every golfer. People come in every size and shape, and we all have different equipment needs. I couldn't play well with Ernie Els's golf clubs, and he probably would be uncomfortable with mine.

If you haven't updated your equipment for a while, here are some ideas to help you find what you need:

Woods

The driver is the king of clubs and the one golfers most love to hit. Every golfer who wants to reach his full potential must find and use the driver best suited to his or her swing.

We all miss fairways. Even PGA tour pros hit only about two out of every three, and the long bombers might miss half or more. To improve your long game, you need to start making *better misses* with the driver. It's no crime to hit in the rough. You still have a chance to recover and make par, or no worse than bogey. However, if you regularly hook, pull, push, or slice your driver out of play, you are defeated before you get off the tee box. We'll cover those problems in Chapter 6.

If you are still trying to drive with a three-wood or uncle Zeb's 1980 persimmon driver, get ready to experience a revolution in your game. With the right driver, you'll discover the joy of shooting for greens from the middle of the fairway instead of chipping out from the woods. You'll also be 20 or more yards farther down the course.

There is a perfect driver out there for everyone. Dozens of companies offer scores of models, lofts, and shafts. The shaft has more effect on your ability to hit good shots than the brand or head size. I suggest that mid and high handicappers use ten degrees or more of loft. These drivers are easier to hit straight and still provide plenty of distance.

Your goal is to hit the ball as far as possible and still make the fairway more than half the time. With your new driver, you will experience better misses. Golf is a game of nonstop mistakes and recoveries. You never "get it down perfectly" like you would a piece of music. Your mistakes just get less punitive and occur less frequently. This translates steadily to improved scores and a lower handicap.

Start out by experimenting with your friends' drivers. Find out what shafts they have. Borrow demo clubs from your golf shop or the local golf store. Get advice from golf store employees. Discuss drivers, shafts, and kick points with a golf pro. Pretty quickly, you will find a driver that fits your swing perfectly. Buy it. You've just cut several strokes off your game.

Update Your Equipment

Higher swing speeds, ninety miles per hour and up, normally are best suited to a stiff shaft. Lower swing speeds take regular, senior, or ladies shafts. Most golfers take a mid-kick shaft, but if you consistently hit the ball too low, try shafts with a low kick point. Likewise, if you have trouble hitting the ball too high, get shafts with a high kick point.

Your driver doesn't have to be brand new. Some golfers buy a new driver every year, and the old one goes back to the store or onto eBay.com. Most golf courses sell used drivers and demos. A good used driver might sell for less than half of its cost new. Models two or three years old will go cheaper than that. Look around. Check on the Internet. Good used drivers are everywhere.

Your fairway woods don't have to be the same brand as your driver. I have used five or six different drivers over the years. I've played with seven and nine-woods. Test out these fairway clubs just as you did your driver. It won't take long to find clubs and shafts that feel and hit just right for you.

You might also try some of the specialty clubs, like rescue clubs and ironwoods. Good golfers are having great success with these hybrids. If cost is a factor, you always have the option of knockoffs or used. You will find these specialty clubs easy to hit and you can use them in place of long irons. Don't buy anything more than two or three years old. Hybrid clubs can improve your golf game, and bargains can be found on every corner.

Irons

Every golfer in this day and age should buy irons that fit his size and swing. Any medium-sized city will have a store that can fit you. A club professional can tell you where you can have this done.

Your irons need to be the right length, have the right shaft, and have the correct lie (angle of the head) for your swing. When the lie is set properly, you have the perfect height relationship between the heel and toe of the iron when you address the ball.

Modern irons are ten times easier to hit than those of a few years back. Be sure to get cavity back irons, and take care to learn the right kick point and flexibility for your swing. Again, test demo clubs from a golf store or pro shop. Find what works best for you. Pay close attention to shaft flexibility. Once you've determined that, test different brands. Many irons, even used ones, can have the lie adjusted to the right degree for your swing.

Just like a new driver, a well-fitting set of irons will improve your game overnight. It will take a little time to find what's right for you, but it's worth it in the long run, and golf is a long term proposition.

The Putter

Putting is a game of confidence, and a putter that gives you confidence is the one you should be using. I keep several putters on hand, and I can always switch if I lose confidence in the one I am using.

While you are in the store testing woods and irons, you should try out different putters. There are dozens of different types, styles, and sizes.

I once asked the pro at a nearby golf club if he switched putters when his went sour. "Yes," he answered. In fact, he had fifty-four putters in his garage. This kid was twenty-seven years old!

As long as your putter is legal, there is no right or wrong. It is just a matter of what feels right and having faith in the putter you're using. When putting trouble comes, changing equipment can help.

Golf Balls

Ask a pro what brand and compression golf ball would best fit your game. Golf balls are so good these days, you can hardly go wrong. Buy the best balls you can afford.

GPS Distance Measuring Systems

GPS distance measuring devices are available for today's golfer and are even allowed in some tournaments. They give you precise distances to the front, middle, and back of every green, plus lay up distances to hazards. These handheld devices are also perfect for practicing distance control short iron shots. They aren't cheap, but the benefits are immeasurable. Thousands of courses are downloadable to these GPS devices. You can also manually set up any course not available online. Check out different brands on the Internet.

POINTS TO REMEMBER

- You can buy a lot of golf game.
- Test drivers until you find one that feels perfect. Used drivers are cheaper and work well. Pay close attention to shaft flexibility and kick point.
- Buy a set of irons specifically fitted to your swing. Get the right shaft flexibility, lie and kick point.
- Confidence in your putter is more important than anything else.
- Find the golf ball that best fits your game.
- Get a golf GPS system if you can afford it.

4

Track Your Progress

You've set a goal and committed to sticking with it. You're playing with the best equipment you can find. Now is the time to start tracking your progress and focusing on weaknesses in your game.

The golf handicap system allows players of all strengths to play a fair game against each another. Better still, it allows you to accurately track your progress as a golfer.

Using the handicap system, you can tell within a shot or two how good you are. You can use it to tell if you are getting better or worse. You can compare your strength to other players.

Your handicap is determined by the number of strokes above or below par you would be expected to shoot in the best ten of your last twenty rounds. It is based on the number of shots you take, in addition to the difficulty of the golf courses you have played in those twenty rounds.

Track Your Progress

Since you only use ten of your previous twenty rounds, a handicap reveals only your *potential* as a golfer.

I've read that the average handicap for male golfers is around sixteen. This typical golfer would be expected to shoot 88 on a par-72 golf course on his best days. This assumes that he takes no mulligans and penalizes himself stroke and distance on out-of-bounds shots and lost balls. He would play all hazard shots by the book and always play the ball as he finds it, without improving the lie. Golfers I've observed don't always play by such strict rules. So while a handicap can be a good indicator of strength, a 16-handicapper who's accustomed to "loose" scoring methods might easily shoot 100 under tournament conditions.

According to a golf magazine article I saw a few years ago, a 36-handicapper would not be expected to hit a single green in regulation during an eighteen-hole round. An 18-handicapper would be expected to hit only three. A 9-handicapper would hit about seven greens, and a 4-handicapper would hit ten. A scratch golfer would be expected to hit about twelve greens in regulation.

The same players would get up and down from off the green in the following percentages: 36-handicapper, 0 percent; 18-handicapper, 17 percent; 9-handicapper, 46 percent; 4-handicapper, 60 percent; scratch golfer, 77 percent.

For sand saves (up and down in two from the sand): 36-handicapper, 0 percent; 18-handicapper, 0 percent; 9-handicapper, 7 percent; 4-handicapper, 31 percent; scratch golfer, 51 percent. Note that the big difference between a single-digit handicapper and scratch golfer is short game skill.

It is more difficult to gauge your putting game accurately. I consider any round with thirty or fewer putts a good putting round. It would be exceptional if I had hit ten or more greens in regulation. With only five or six greens in regulation, I would hope to take no more than thirty putts.

When you count your putts, tally any shot hit with the putter from off the green as a chip. Only putts from the actual putting surface count as putts.

Another way to gauge your putting round is simply to count three-putts. You hope to have none, but more than two three-putts in eighteen holes is a round killer.

Keep track of all your numbers for fairways, greens in regulation, up and downs, and putting, then compare them to the above standards.

It's easy to isolate your weaknesses when you have this knowledge. If one area of your game goes bad for a single round, forget it. But if you notice for three or four consecutive rounds that you are struggling with a particular aspect of your game, determine why and go to work on the problem. If you can't figure out how to get past your troubles, take a lesson from your pro. The good news is that most golf troubles are easily fixed. The bad news is that fresh problems are always coming your way. You have to learn to deal with each difficulty as it shows up. Even Tiger Woods takes lessons and gets fixes. You have to be willing to do the same.

Only by being constantly aware of where you are weak can you improve your golf. As soon as you fix one aspect of your game, find the next problem and solve it. Winning golfers are constantly observing their games, focusing on their weaknesses, and working to get better. Don't fall into the trap of working exclusively on "the swing." If you're a high handicapper, you have to regularly practice shots of 35-100 yards.

The more you concentrate on your weaknesses, the quicker you get better at golf. Keep doing this, week after week and month after month. You will be astounded at how fast you progress.

I have for years used the Yahoo.com golf handicap tracker to record my scores. The Internet is full of golf handicap trackers. Sign up for one and begin posting your scores online.

I use the following guidelines for keeping my handicap: (1) only eighteen-hole rounds count; (2) I don't post a score the first time I play a course; (3) as long as my handicap stays below 10, double bogey is the maximum number I write down; and (4) in cold and windy weather (wind chill below 40), I don't post my scores.

Use the method shown below when scoring your own rounds for handicap purposes. The USGA uses a system called ESC, or Equitable Stroke Control system. It limits the number of strokes you can take on any hole for handicap purposes. This keeps a blowup hole from destroying what might otherwise have been a decent round. It also prevents abuse by sandbaggers.

Handicap	Maximum score per hole
Below 10	Double Bogey
10-19.9	7
20-29.9	8
30-39 .9	9
40 and higher	10

Follow the above guidelines and record your rounds, regardless of how good or how bad. Compare your drives in the fairway, greens in regulation, up and downs, sand saves, and putting figures with those given earlier in this chapter.

I sometimes play golf in the dead of winter when it's impossible to score well. There's little grass, the ball is like a rock, club distances shorten by about 15 percent, and here in Oklahoma, we usually have strong wind to add to the misery. Posting rounds in this type of weather artificially inflates your handicap.

Keeping records forces you to concentrate on your weaknesses. If you are missing fairways, work on setup and aim; if you are missing greens, practice your irons and be sure you're aiming correctly. If you seldom get up and down from areas close to the green, go to work on chipping, pitching, and distance control wedges. If you are missing short putts or you three-putt too often, practice your putting. If you don't know how to fix what's wrong, take a lesson from your pro.

When you post your rounds for handicap purposes, play by the rules. Don't take mulligans. Count stroke and distance when you go out-of-bounds or lose a ball. Post every round you play and not just the ones that help your handicap.

It's essential to be aware of what's costing you strokes and directing your efforts to that phase of your game. It's not hard if you have a goal in mind.

This is how you go from hacker to real golfer.

POINTS TO REMEMBER

- Your handicap is based on the average of your best ten scores in the last twenty rounds you played. It shows your *potential* as a golfer.
- A single-digit handicapper will hit about half the fairways, half the greens and get up and down (including from sand) three or four times out of ten.
- Improving golfers need to keep a handicap, track their games, notice their weaknesses and regularly work to improve them.

5

Don't Be a Perfectionist

Golf is not a sport for perfectionists. Even the best round of a golfer's life is not perfectly played. Annika Sorenstam says a perfect round of golf is 54, all birdies, but she has never come close to shooting it.

The process of improving your golf game consists of increasing, through intelligent practice, the number of shots you have a chance to confidently execute – and the most important skill is the ability to control distance.

Developing players need to learn to pick the right shot to hit in any of the varying circumstances they might encounter in a round of golf. They have to know their own capabilities and adapt their play to those capabilities. Finally, they must have realistic handicap goals and be able to see themselves reaching those goals.

Every golfer seems to want to "get the swing down" and hit the driver 300 yards before starting to work on wedge distance control, chips, or pitches. That's putting the cart before the horse. I've had numerous arguments with golf friends who spend all their time working on "the swing" before developing other important parts of the game. This erroneous compulsion never seems to end, and "the swing" is never quite good enough to allow time to work on distance control, chipping, and putting. If these golfers do finally decide to practice short shots, they think thirty minutes a year is overdoing it.

A 60-yard pitching wedge is easier to hit than a full-swing four-iron. You can learn to hit the ball squarely with these shorter swings. These are the shots that quickly improve your scoring. I get tired of hearing, "I'm not a good enough ball striker to hit the distance control shots (got to get "the swing" down first!). And so it goes. After five, ten, or twenty years, these golfers are still trying to break 100 or 90. They continue to work on getting "the swing" down so they can finally get ready to learn to use their wedges and putter.

Ralph Waldo Emerson wisely stated, "We are always getting ready to live, but never living." Translated to golf terms, we could analogize: "We are always getting ready to practice wedges and putting, but never practicing them." You don't actually get the short shots "down," either. You simply practice them occasionally – not hours a day or even hours a week. It doesn't take that much time. One positive, well planned hour of practice every week can change your golf game.

When you have practiced distance control wedge shots, you have experience and a swing to fit varying distances to the green. It doesn't mean you'll always hit the green and one-putt, but the chances are good that you'll get the ball to the hole and be closer than if you'd never practiced a shot of that distance. When you've made a close friend of the 50-yard pitching wedge, it's there for you when you need it.

Consistently adding to the number of shots you know and have a fair chance of executing is how you rapidly improve. As you increase the number of different shots you can hit, confidence will replace fear. For most situations you face on the course, you'll have a practiced shot, ready to play. That preparedness must result in lower scores.

Don't Be A Perfectionist

You will never be able to hit every green in regulation or hit every 75-yard wedge shot to within eight feet of the flagstick. But if you've done it in practice, you've improved your chances of successfully executing it when it counts. Strive not for perfection, but to keep improving your odds. Perfectionists have no business on a golf course.

Week by week, and month by month, keep adding to your arsenal, one shot at a time. Before long, you'll have a known shot for any approach to the green.

You won't have it "down," but you'll have greatly increased your chances to score well.

POINTS TO REMEMBER

- You cannot be a perfectionist in golf. You'll never "get it down."
- With correct practice, you can continually improve your *chances* to shoot better scores.
- It is easier to learn to make solid contact with a short wedge shot than with a full swing.
- Golfers seem always to be "getting ready" to practice wedges and putting, but never practicing them.
- Keep adding to the number of shots you have a reasonable *chance* of hitting successfully, and your scores will quickly improve.

6

Long Game Success

This chapter is not about swing lessons, it's about playing better golf with the swing you already have. It presents sensible and practical ideas through which you can make immediate improvement in your ball striking and long game results.

Swing lessons are the job of your local professional. Your pro will be happy to observe, evaluate, and address your individual problems and idiosyncrasies. No golf book can do that. In an hour's time a pro can identify and correct temporary setup or swing problems and have you hitting the ball well. You don't have to take a lesson every week or even every month. I never did. When I did run into difficulties I couldn't work out myself, I sought a professional, and I always got my money's worth.

Long Game Success

The long game should be the least punitive part of golf, because you usually have a chance to recover from mistakes. A bad short shot, on the other hand, almost always costs a full stroke, sometimes two. If you hit your drive into the rough on a par four, a good recovery shot can still put the ball on the green and result in a par. Even if you can't make it onto the green, you still can make par with a good chip, putt, or sand shot. The inaccurate drive didn't matter. You probably only lost a chance to make birdie.

****

Don't try to do everything in this chapter at once. Read through it at least twice and get the ideas clearly in your head. Then start applying them to your game, one at a time. It won't take long since every step is simple. It's easy to read these lines, pass judgment one way or another, and go on playing golf the same way you always did. Don't do that. The ideas have to be *applied* to yield any benefit. Start out by moving to the right tees for your length. Next, learn to aim correctly. That will knock strokes off your game immediately. Once you can reliably aim straight, move on to the other points.

Give serious thought and effort to the winning ideas in this chapter. They're yours for the taking, and they'll make golf more fun than you can imagine.

Learn to Aim

Incorrect setup and aim cause high-handicap golfers more misery and embarrassment than any other mistake. Again and again, I have watched high handicappers meticulously take their grip, adjust ball position, make careful practice swings, and do whatever else they've just read about in a golf magazine, and then walk to the ball and unconsciously aim twenty degrees left or right of their intended target line. The ball ends up in the sand, in the water, or out of bounds, and blame gets assigned to a bad swing.

Poor golfers always believe they are setting up and aiming straight ("Of course I know how to aim a golf shot!"), but they're wrong, dead wrong. From a right angle, what their eyes and mind perceive as straight can be miles from reality. Imagine a baseball pitcher trying to throw a fastball over home plate with his feet aimed twenty degrees left or right of the correct position. Golfers try to play from these same contorted positions all day long without even knowing it. The body aims one way, and the mind tells the arms to swing another.

Aim is the most ignored fundamental in all of golf. Bad golfers seldom consider it when they practice (too busy getting "the swing" down). I'll never forget watching my first teacher, Dennis Bowman, practicing alone at the Cherry Springs range with his feet lined up to an aim club. PGA pros do it. Tour players do it. You need to do it, too.

Before you hit any practice shot, pick a small target down range and place a club on the ground with the grip end pointed directly at your target. Next, lay another club parallel to and about twelve inches inside (closer to your feet) the first club. The second club is aimed "parallel left" of the target.

Now align your toes with the "parallel left" club, remove the first club, and get ready to hit. This correctly aligned "parallel left" position (Figure 1) will probably feel awkward at first, but do it every single time you hit a ball at the practice range.

Set up with your feet, hips, and shoulders parallel to the alignment club. Each foot should be the same distance from your aim club. With your feet aimed parallel left (slightly left) of the target, the swing plane of your club will be directly at the target. Open shoulders (aimed left) can cause a slice or pull, closed shoulders (aimed right) can cause a hook or push. Have a friend or your pro observe your stance from behind to be sure you have lined everything up correctly. The more awkward and uncomfortable this feels, the more faulty your past setup position has been, and the more benefit you will ultimately derive from learning correct alignment.

Form the habit of aligning yourself with the aim club every time you hit practice balls. Do this no matter what club you are hitting. Habit will soon start lining you up correctly on the course.

I was never a ball beater at the range. With my distressed back, I seldom hit more than 150 practice balls in a week's time, but I always used an aim club. Before every shot I picked a target. Then I would get

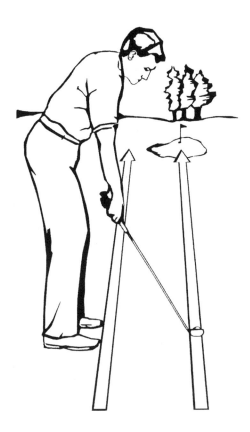

(Figure 1)
Parallel Left

behind the ball and choose an aim spot on the ground. Only then did I walk to the ball and swing. I knew I was lining up and aiming correctly and I took that capability to the course.

Jack Nicklaus advocates the aim spot routine. Before setting up, Nicklaus would get behind the ball and pick a spot on the ground a few inches ahead of his ball. It could be a blade of grass, a leaf, or an anthill. The spot he picked was on a direct line with his intended target. Once he had picked his alignment target, he simply walked to the ball and lined everything up with that spot and made his swing.

Every golfer must constantly be aware of alignment. If you line up left or right of your target, your subconscious knows it and tries to correct your club path. With your feet and body lined up one direction and your arms trying to swing another, you're engaged in nothing more than flailing.

If you're a high handicapper, you don't know how to align and aim straight. If you don't learn anything else from this book, learn to align and aim. You aren't doing it now; believe me. Unless you regularly practice with an aim club and always pick an aim point on the ground in front of your ball, you don't aim straight.

Watch the PGA tour pros on television. Nearly all of them get behind the ball and line up the shot before walking to the ball and setting up. If these guys have to do it, so do you. I repeat, don't *ever* practice without using an alignment club. Don't *ever* hit another shot on the course without picking a target spot in front of your ball and lining up your clubface with that spot.

Fortunately, most of the prerequisites for hitting a good golf shot are met before you ever start your backswing. Learn to align and aim correctly and you'll start hitting a lot more successful shots. It will probably feel very different at first, but incorporate this into your routine and never stop doing it.

Play from the Tee Box Best Suited to Your Length

For most golfers, the long game is the most fun part of golf. Everyone loves to hit a high drive down the middle and place their approach shot on the green. You have a chance to do that only if you are playing from the right tees.

A golfer who averages less than 180 yards off the tee should be playing from the front tees (course length under 5,200 yards). Players who drive 180-225 yards are best suited for the senior tees (5200-6100 yards. Only golfers who consistently hit the ball over 225 yards off the tee should be playing from the 6100-plus-yards and longer tees.

Golf is hard enough even when you have a chance to hit the green in regulation and two-putt for par. Playing tees that are too long for your game can add a dozen or more strokes to your score. Golf courses have different tees for a reason, and that reason is to make the game fair and fun for everybody.

If you're consistently unable to reach the green in regulation figures (one shot on a par three, two on a par four, and three on a par five), move up. If you have to hit three-wood to the green on every par four, the course is too long. Don't let an inflated ego ruin your golf. Many men are afraid of how they might look playing from shorter tees, but nothing looks sillier than a golfer with a 180-yard drive trying to play a 6500-yard golf course. There is no shame in playing from the senior, or even the front tees. Different tees are there to give every golfer a chance to reach the green in regulation.

On the Downswing, Return your Hands to their Original Setup Position

A conspicuous difference between experienced golfers and weak amateurs is the ability of good players to return their hands (at impact) to the exact same position they were in at setup. Weak golfers bring their hands down farther away from the body – sometimes as much as four or five inches farther out. This guarantees an over-the-top, glancing blow, and with it, chaotic and unpredictable ball striking. My instructor, Dennis Bowman, says this suggestion has improved the ball striking of his students more quickly than anything else, and he has seen it work hundreds of times.

Notice the angle of your club shaft at setup. That's where it should be when you strike the ball. Ponder this and practice making slow swings without a ball, returning your hands to their original setup position as they pass through the bottom of the swing arc.

Strike the Ball with a Descending Blow

In order to hit beautiful, high golf shots, you have to strike the ball with a descending blow. This applies not only to iron shots, but to fairway woods and hybrids, as well as to pitches and chips. Only with your driver off a tee do you hit the ball with an upward strike. Take a look at Figure 2. The club strikes down and through the ball before it makes a divot in front of where the ball originally lay. Though it seems to defy logic, a descending blow will give you more height and controlled distance than any other type of contact. The golf ball is compressed against the club and ground. It then rolls up the face of the club and expands, flying high and far with backspin. All good golfers strike the ball in this manner. If you have trouble with this, focus on striking downward, just below the equator of the ball. Picture swinging *through* the ball, making a divot in front of where it lay. As with every golf shot, think *balanced* and *smooth* as you practice this powerful descending stroke.

Impact tape is a handy tool to help you develop skill in striking a golf ball. The tape is placed on the face of your club, indicates exactly where your club has struck the ball and guides you to make instant corrections. It's a great way to learn to hit the ball squarely. Every developing golfer should practice with impact tape. If your warm up shots before a round are flying wild, a piece of impact tape and minor corrections can quickly put you back on track. You can find impact tape at most golf stores or on the Internet.

If you find yourself in an extended bad patch of ball striking, your rhythm is probably off and you need to temporarily gear back. Take more club (five-iron instead of seven, for example) and make three-quarter swings. It's easier to hit these "punch" shots solidly, though they will fly lower and without as much spin. Make less than full swings with your driver. A three-quarter driver does not travel too much shorter than a full shot, and it's more dependable. Play these relaxed, smooth, and balanced shorter shots for a while and your full swing will soon return as good as ever.

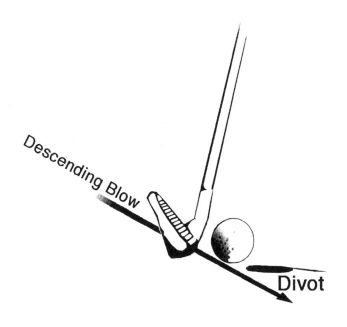

(Figure 2)
The Descending Blow

When your ball striking goes on vacation, a golf professional can usually get you back on the right track in a single lesson. It's often just a minor setup or aim problem.

Use Swing Maintenance Devices

If you've played enough golf to become a 25–30 handicapper, you've no doubt spent plenty of time studying "the swing." You've probably taken lessons, read golf magazines, watched the Golf Channel, and received swing advice from your friends.

"The swing" is a whimsical acquaintance. One day it happily serves you; the next day it's nowhere to be found. Once you've learned how to set up and aim correctly, you can keep your swing in tune with the training aids listed below. What's great about these products is that you can develop and maintain good swing fundamentals without investing hours and hours of practice time. I use all three, and I believe they will benefit any golfer who uses them. You can find them on the Internet.

ReFiner or Medicus hinged practice clubs

These swing-practice clubs are built with one or two hinges in the shaft that break on out-of-tempo or off-plane swings. Well-known instructors highly recommend them. Millions have been sold, and for good reason – they work. The clubs can be carried in your golf bag or conveniently used indoors. I've used a single-break ReFiner five-iron for years, and I like to make ten to fifteen smooth swings before heading to the first tee.

Momentus weighted swing club

The Momentus is a heavy practice club that helps ingrain a correct swing path and consistency. It only takes a few swings to experience the correct "in the slot" feeling and a good wrist snap at the bottom. Extra weight has the advantage of strengthening golf muscles and the pre-molded grip is an additional benefit. I swing mine ten to fifteen times before practice or play. You can find knock offs of weighted swing training clubs in major discount stores.

Inside Approach

This device teaches the correct "inside" swing path, helping cure the dreaded slice and adding yardage to every club. It consists of a tube-shaped cushion held horizontally about six inches above the ground by a plastic stand. Practice consists of hitting a golf ball placed under the device without striking the cushion. This can be accomplished only with an inside-out swing path. A swing from the outside will cause the club to crash into the cushion, which safely separates from the holder without damaging the device or golf club.

Learn the Correct Grip

Eighty per cent of golfers slice the ball. Slicing is the result of an open club face at impact. Although many mistakes can cause this, two of the most common are lining up incorrectly and using a grip that is too weak. This holds true regardless of whether you use the overlapping, interlocking, or ten-finger grip.

By weak, I don't mean how tightly one grips the club; I mean that the V's formed by the thumb and first finger point too far to the left. With a friend or your pro watching, take your normal grip and see where your V's point. The most common mistake is for the left hand V to point up the left arm to the left ear or left shoulder. To correct this, set up normally, and without moving the club, rotate your left hand to the right until the V between your left thumb and forefinger points at your right ear. Next, rotate the V of your right hand to also point at the right ear. With a correct grip, you should be able to see two knuckles of each hand (Figure 3).

Try hitting some balls with this grip. It might feel strange at first, but your left-to-right ball flight should correct itself. If you find that you are hooking the ball, rotate both V's very slightly back to the left. Be certain your feet and shoulders are aligned and aimed correctly. Continue experimenting and adjusting until you find the ball flight you want. Then, *memorize* the exact position of your hands and check for the correct grip before every shot.

Often, players will learn the correct grip but forget it during a serious round. By the time they get to the back nine, they're back to the old grip, and in the heat of the moment, can't remember why they are slicing again. Make a grip check part of your pre-shot routine. A correct grip will soon become second nature and your slicing will be reduced to a minimum.

Poor golf shots are caused by gripping the club too tightly. Gripping too hard with one hand or the other will surely cause erratic ball flights. Johnny Miller says in an instructional videotape that many golfers would be surprised at how lightly he grips the golf club. Relax and hold the club just tightly enough for control.

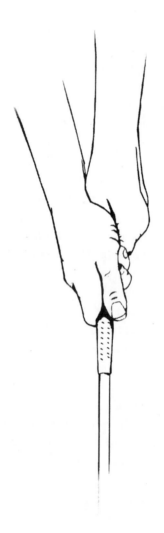

(Figure 3)
V's point to golfer's right ear

Placement of the V's toward the golfer's right (strong grip), will draw or hook. V's to the golfer's left (weak grip) will fade or slice.

Long Game Success

Think "Balance"

At one point early in my golf days, I was having a terrible time hitting fairway woods. I'd hit fat, thin, off the heel, and off the toe. I was utterly unable to hit a good shot off the ground with any wood.

During a visit to an out-of-town course, I decided to take a lesson from the club pro. I described my troubles and the pro sent me to the range to warm up. When he arrived a few minutes later, he asked me to hit some balls with my three-wood. It took about four swings for him to diagnose and solve my problem. "You're off balance as you strike the ball," he said. "Think only about stability and balance, and swing with eighty percent power." That was it. I immediately began thinking "balance," and all of a sudden my shots started going long and straight. I hit eight or ten pretty shots in a row and he asked, "Anything else?" I answered no, handed him $35, and he returned to the pro shop. It was the best money I ever spent.

That lesson was years ago, but to this day, whenever I prepare to hit a fairway wood, I think "balance." It's a good thought for any golf shot.

Avoid Swaying on the Backswing

Swaying the hips to the right on the backswing is another insidious fault, resulting in poor ball striking and power loss.

Golfers with a sway problem erroneously place the weight of their right foot toward the *outside* of this foot, allowing the hips and right knee to move right on the backswing, a power killer. Weight belongs on the *left* side of the right foot.

There's an easy fix. Set up on the range and place a golf ball under the right side of your right foot. This creates a sway-proof foundation and keeps weight on the left side of that foot. Now hit a few balls. As you make your backswing, notice how you rotate against a firm and stable right leg. That's what you want to feel on the course.

You can practice this at home. Grab your five-iron and set up to swing. Put a ball under the right side of your right foot. Now place the back of an open folding chair an inch from your right hip. The back of the chair should extend no higher than your hip and allow a full swing.

Next, without a ball, make a few swings, not allowing your right hip to sway into the chair. You'll feel a coil against a stable right leg. This helps keep your head and body steady throughout the swing, a key to good ball striking. Rotating the heel of your right foot slightly to the right can also improve stability. Power and accuracy will immediately improve when you take this to the course.

Stay Behind the Ball

If you have difficulty getting height on your tee shots, be certain your left ear is to the right side (away from the target) of the ball at address. This means that your upper body is leaning to the right. The easiest way to achieve this position is to drop the right shoulder two inches. Watch a slow motion front view of any tour pro's swing and you will observe this right shoulder low position. When the club makes impact with the ball, the head is still behind the ball and the upper body is leaning to the right (Figure 4).

Try hitting a few balls from this position, left ear staying right of the ball all the way through impact. As you make your swing, focus on your right ear lobe and *don't let it move* until the right shoulder brings your head up. This is called staying behind the ball, and it works terrifically to produce long and solid shots, particularly with the driver.

Swing at 80 Percent of Full Power for Maximum Distance and Accuracy

This was Moe Norman's decree, and Moe was the best ball striker who ever lived. If you learn to swing at 80 percent power, you will hit the best long shots of your life. You can prove this at the range. And watch how *straight* you hit the shots as well as how far. Look at the ball before you swing, and like Sam Snead used to do, say, "Don't worry honey; I'm not going to hurt you." This thought helps take the "kill it" instinct out of your mind and allows for a smooth swing.

(Figure 4)
The Post-Impact Position
Staying Behind the Ball

Learn the Post-Impact Position and Practice It Before Every Round.

I use a TIVO recording system for my DirecTV, and I can stop and repeat live action when I watch golf. When I see a tour professional hit a great shot, I run the recorder back and watch the setup and swing in slow motion. I can even watch one frame at a time.

After the pro has hit the ball, the eyes continue to stare at the spot where the ball was sitting until the trailing shoulder brings the head up. I call the Post-Impact Position the point at which you have already hit the ball and your hands have moved twelve to fifteen inches past the impact position. At this point, your head should still be waiting for the right shoulder to bring it up.

Without a club, take a very slow practice swing and stop your hands twelve to fifteen inches past the impact point. Keep your head perfectly still and looking down. Feel and remember this position.

When you get to the course, do this exercise slowly at least a dozen times, with or without a club before you hit balls or begin play. Get used to this position. Think about it. Feel it. Hands forward, head steady and waiting for the right shoulder to bring it up. Keep the Post-Impact Position in mind. It's another key to solid ball striking.

Relax the Hands and Arms Before You Swing.

Take a hint from tour pro Fred Couples. As he prepares to take a shot, notice how he rolls his shoulders and shakes his arms. Fred is relaxing these muscles. He has one of the most relaxed looking swings in golf, and he is an exceptionally long hitter.

As you set up, consciously relax your hands and arms. Next, take a practice swing and feel the club whip through at the bottom. In this relaxed mode, line up, and take the shot. You will have higher clubhead speed, greater accuracy, and more distance with relaxed muscles and an eighty percent swing than you could ever achieve by swinging from the heels with gritted teeth. Don't try so hard – just pick a target and let it happen.

Watch the swings of tour professionals Ernie Els, Retief Goosen and Couples. These professionals are relaxed and smooth, as though they were practicing on the range. And they all hit the ball a mile.

You want your subconscious mind to direct your relaxed hands and arms to send the ball to your target. If you grip the club tightly, trying to kill the ball and control everything yourself, you override the subconscious. Bad shots are the inevitable result. You must think about your target, give up control, and have some faith to play this game well.

In Your "Mind's Eye," See the Ball Going to Your Target

This is another Jack Nicklaus lesson, and he was the best in the world at visualizing his shots. It focuses your mind on what you want, not what you fear.

Nicklaus explained that before a full shot, he would first see the ball landing and rolling to his target. Then he would picture the trajectory that the ball would have to take to land where he had selected. Next, he pictured what swing his body had to produce in order to make this exact shot.

Nicklaus held a clear picture of what he *wanted,* and then let his subconscious take over and make the desired shot. If you focus on a spot in the fairway or on the green, chances are you will hit the ball there. If you picture hitting into a bunker, pond, or out of bounds, the odds are good that you will hit that shot. Whatever you are thinking about as you swing, positive or negative, will certainly affect the flight of your ball.

Monitor Ball Position

Most golfers have occasional trouble with ball position. Round by round, the ball creeps slightly forward or back in the setup stance without the player's awareness. This can create chaos in ball striking, even when the golfer is doing everything else right.

To determine correct ball position, take a few practice swings, note the spot where the club strikes the ground and make sure the ball is situated where the divot will be made in front of where the ball originally lay.

POINTS TO REMEMBER

- You can recover from long-game mistakes and still make par.
- Learn how to line up straight and aim.
- Play from tees best suited to your length, not your age.
- On the downswing, return your hands to their original setup position.
- Strike the ball with a descending blow.
- Use swing maintenance devices.
- Learn the correct grip.
- Think "balance."
- Avoid swaying on the backswing.
- Stay behind the ball and keep your right ear lobe perfectly still when you swing.
- Swing at 80 per cent of full power for maximum distance and accuracy.
- Learn the "Post Impact Position" and practice it before every round.
- Relax the hands and arms before you swing.
- See in your "mind's eye" the ball going to your target before you start the backswing.
- Monitor ball position.

7

Distance Control –
The Secret of Golf

Stop the presses! Take a deep breath. Your life as a golfer is about to change forever – and change greatly for the better. The lessons in this chapter are going to turn your double bogeys into bogeys and your bogeys into pars and birdies. What you learn here can drop your scores and handicap as much as ten or fifteen strokes. It happened to me and it makes this the most important chapter in the entire book.

Be aware that every tour pro, club champion and low handicap golfer has a sound game from 100 yards and closer. There's simply no way around it, and if you want to go from hacker to golfer you have to know the shots taught in this chapter.

I can hear that little voice in your head screaming, "Short game? NO! NO! I'll work on that later. I'm not ready. I'll practice that when my swing comes around. I'm not good enough yet." This kind of thinking is illogical. Recognize this important point: you build your swing and your game around these shots. You learn to hit the golf ball squarely with these shots. You develop good rhythm and smoothness with these shorter shots.

Learning what's in this chapter will take less time than you think, so don't create a false mental obstacle about the short game. Stay positive. This is going to turn you into a real golfer. You know – shooting in the 70s, collecting the money after the round, having a single-digit handicap – those little benefits. You *can* do this and you must do it. Once you experience the instant payback that comes from hitting accurate short shots, you'll look forward to practicing them.

Golf is a game of distance control. The ability to control how far one hits the ball, particularly from inside 100 yards, is the defining difference between a real golfer and a hacker.

In a full round of golf, you'll hit only eighteen shots where distance doesn't matter; fourteen tee shots and four second shots to the par fives. With virtually every other shot, you are trying to stop the ball somewhere on the green or at the hole. Even short par fours and second shots on the par fives can require a controlled lay-up distance. Carefully ponder this fact – four out of every five shots you hit require distance control, including the two-foot putt that can be left short or spun out with careless play.

You have to know the full-swing distance of every club in your bag. Without this knowledge, you're not really playing golf. You're mindlessly whacking balls around a pasture and hoping.

How do you know which club to hit when your ball is, for example, 125 yards from the green, if you don't know your club distances? Do you hit an easy seven-iron, a smooth nine-iron or a hard wedge? It's different for everybody. Playing experience and practice on a well-marked range quickly teach you the distance you hit each club.

High handicappers are notorious for hitting their approach shots far short of the flagstick and often short of the green itself. They make the mistake of assuming that they will hit the maximum distance the club in their hand ever produced for them instead of what's about average.

These golfers have to learn to take enough club to get the ball to the green, and hopefully pin high, on their first approach shot.

The closer you get to the hole, the more vital distance control becomes. From closer in, you can learn to put the ball next to the flagstick and one-putt, saving a full stroke. That means learning to hit the ball precise distances when you are less than a full swing away from the green. At worst, you want to hit the green and two-putt from inside 100 yards. That usually takes double-bogey out of the equation. To have a real chance to one-putt, you are going to have to be able to hit your wedge shots to within eight feet or less, at least some of the time. Why eight feet? Because that gives you a genuine chance to one-putt and save a full stroke. Approach shots landing outside eight feet will normally result in a two-putt.

If you watch golf on television, you get a quick education on distance control from the tour pros. They never hit any shot that can reach the hole without verifying the *exact* distance with their caddy. What more proof do you need of the importance of distance control?

Most golfers can tell you about how far they expect to hit a full shot with their six-iron, nine-iron, or sand wedge, but they seem clueless when confronted with a 40-yard pitch to the flagstick. I have had some pretty fair players tell me that they would rather hit a full shot from 125 yards than face a 40-yard pitch to the green. I don't buy into that. You can get the ball closer to the hole from 40 yards if you have spent any time at all on your wedge game.

How do you learn to hit a golf ball 40 yards, or 50, or 75? You must have a wedge in your hand and have a practiced swing with that wedge that you know will produce the required distance. Eyeballing and guessing leads to wasted strokes.

In order to score well, you must be able to hit your wedges with precise swings to produce any distance from 35 to 100 yards in length. Pitches shorter than 35 yards are covered in Chapter 8, *On and Around the Green*. In early 2000, when I first learned these shots and became able to hit the golf ball a precise distance from within 100 yards of a green, I experienced the quickest and most dramatic improvement of my life (see my charted handicap near the front of the book). The appealing factor was that it took little time and effort to learn it. When I was trying to eyeball distances to the green, guessing what club to use, and then figuring how hard to hit the ball, my results were dismal. The art of controlling distance from close in was a total mystery to me.

My best rounds in those days were around 90 and I usually shot in the 90–100 range. Shortly after discovering the technique for hitting the ball a precise distance from 100 yards and closer, I began scoring in the mid to low 80s, and my handicap dropped to around 12 or 13. Soon after that, I broke 80 for the first time. The wedge shots I had learned made all the difference in the world. For the first time in my life, from short range I was able to match a specific swing to a specific distance. My driving, putting, chipping, and sand play had not significantly changed during these months. The desired result came solely from learning the distance wedge game.

If you dread shots under 100 yards and usually take four or five shots to get down from these distances, what you learn in this chapter will revitalize your golf game. You'll soon find yourself licking your chops when you have a short wedge to the green. You'll consider it a scoring opportunity, a chance to make birdie or save par with a one-putt. You'll be confident of getting down in three shots and playing to get down in two. That's how good golfers think. This confidence takes a lot of pressure off your long game.

I first studied these techniques in *Dave Pelz's Short Game Bible.* Pelz's book is like an encyclopedia and can overwhelm you at first, but you can bypass much of it and go straight to Chapter 5 (*How to Score*) and Chapter 6 (*Distance Wedges*), followed by a review of Chapter 12, (*Secrets of the Short Game*), a handy summary near the end of the book.

Pelz successfully tested his methods on some of the best players in the world. He relates how he taught PGA tour players Tom Kite, Jim Simons, Tom Jenkins, and LPGA pro Jan Stephenson to strengthen their wedge games. After working with Dave Pelz, these professionals rapidly began scoring better and earning top money on their respective tours.

Below is a quick overview of the distance wedge system that you can use to transform your own game. Don't let the "I can't do it" sign block you. You don't need to work more on "the swing" to be able to do this. That's a lame, high-handicapper excuse. Don't be afraid to get out of your comfort zone. If you want to be a real golfer, you *have* to learn these shots, so stay positive and begin now. Don't put it off. It's easier than you think. Get the equipment you need and find a place to learn these distance control shots. It won't take long and massive benefits will quickly come your way.

****

You need to carry at least three wedges; pitching wedge, sand wedge, and lob wedge. You'll have to learn to hit finesse shots with these wedges from any distance from 100 down to 35 yards. If you don't have a lob wedge, add a sixty-degree club to your bag. Give up your three- or four-iron. The extra wedge is far more valuable for scoring. Dave Pelz even advocates a sixty-four-degree wedge.

The idea behind utilizing these wedges is to learn three swings (in addition to the full swing) and three precise distances you hit each wedge. You must learn to use the same rhythm for each swing and make the swing with as little hand action as possible. The beauty of this system is that you don't have to be perfect. With a little practice you can learn to control distance reliably on any short shot to the green. It's like adding six or seven new clubs to your bag.

Imagine the face of a clock with a golfer addressing a ball super-imposed over the clock (Figure 5). Now let us suppose that the golfer has a pitching wedge and a full shot with this club produces a distance of 100 yards. In order to hit the ball half of this distance, 50 yards, the golfer makes what we call a 7:30 swing. In order to hit the ball three-quarters of this distance, or 75 yards, the golfer must make what we call a 9:00 swing. The 10:30 swing will produce a distance of about 90 percent of a full swing, but it is still called a finesse swing.

What do we mean by 7:30, 9:00, and 10:30 swings? A 7:30 swing means that the golfer makes his backswing to the 7:30 position on the clock face with the *hands,* (not the club head), then makes the swing and follows through. If he/she hits the full wedge 100 yards, this shot will travel around 50 yards.

This system works well for every iron in your bag. If you hit a full five-iron 160 yards, your 7:30 swing with that club will travel half of that distance, or 80 yards, a 9:00 swing will go 75 percent of that distance or around 120 yards. This is valuable information if you have 120 yards to the green and you plan to punch under a tree branch with a five-iron. You don't have to guess what swing to make. The half and three-quarter shots with the longer irons are also ideal in windy conditions when you have to keep the ball low. If you apply the above formula, you will be pleased with how accurately you control distance on longer shots. You should never hit any shot, long or short, without knowing ahead of time what club and what swing will produce the distance you want the ball to travel. There is no better feeling than hitting a 75-yard wedge shot precisely 75 yards and watching the ball settle next to the flagstick, leaving a certain one-putt. I'd take that over a 300-yard drive any day of the week.

Learning the distance wedge shot is easy. Before we start, though, understand that you are required to hit the ball with a descending blow. No scooping allowed. No hitting the ground behind the ball. If you try to hit these shots with a scooping motion, you will usually hit a disappointing pop fly that travels half the distance to the hole and wastes a full stroke. Hit the ball first with a descending blow before your club hits the ground. If you need height on the shot, use a more lofted wedge and let the club get the ball in the air. That's what wedges are designed to do, and they don't need your help. Any divot you make should be in front (target side) of where the ball originally lay.

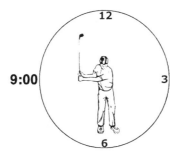

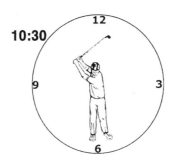

(Figure 5)
Three Magical Swings

Keep the ball back in your stance. If you put it forward, you risk hitting the shot fat. I found that if I moved it back a half-inch to an inch, I was more likely to hit the ball with a descending blow – insurance against the scoop. I get more solid hits, and I seldom leave them short.

I realize your golf time is limited and you'd rather be playing golf when you're at the course, but I implore you to stop and utilize the four hours it takes to play eighteen holes and learn three measured swings and their exact distances for each of your three wedges. You can complete this in one afternoon and be a far better golfer that same day.

To start, you need a practice area that will allow you to hit up to 100 yards to a target. Ideally, you will have both fairway and rough grass for practice. If your practice area doesn't have markers, make your own using an electrical cord or a piece of rope marked in 5 and 10-yard increments. Do whatever you have to do to determine the precise distances you'll be hitting your wedges.

Stand 50 yards from the target, take out your pitching wedge, and make a few 7:30 practice swings. Be aware that this means your hands go back to the 7:30 position on the clock face. Always practice with an aim club. Point the grip of the aim club very slightly left of your target. If you line your feet directly at the target, the club face will be aimed off to the right. Line your toes up even with the aim club to assure correct alignment. Then flare your left foot about 20 degrees toward the target. The ball should be no farther back than one inch to the right of center in your stance. Keep slightly more weight on your left side, maybe 55–45 percent. This will minimize the chance of a scoop.

Make a practice swing or two. Remember your *hands* are going back to the 7:30 position (see Figure 5). This should produce somewhere between 40 and 60 yards with your pitching wedge, maybe less if you're a short hitter. Now take the shot, follow through, and watch the ball fly to the target. If your 7:30 pitching wedge shots are falling way short of 50 yards, you may be decelerating or scooping. Hit down and follow through.

Pelz recommends that you weaken your grip by pointing both V's (between the thumbs and index fingers) at your nose. When I first started practicing this, that grip seemed awkward and uncomfortable, so I tried using a more normal grip. It worked fine, and I've continued to use my regular grip to this day.

Let your hands and arms swing rhythmically back and through, without "slapping" at the ball with your wrists. Relax and stay down through impact. Make the follow-through longer than the backswing. Watch the ball land in order to get maximum feedback and feel. Your goal is to get the ball to within eight feet of the hole. Hit at least twenty-five balls and note how many (if any) you get to within this range. If you were consistently long or short of the target, move closer to or farther from the target. You are trying to determine the distance you hit the pitching wedge with a 7:30 swing. Stay aware of your exact distance from the target. It will do you no good to eyeball distances and try to match swings. Precise yardage measurements and matching swings are essential for this training.

Go through the procedure again, noting how many of the twenty-five balls you get within eight feet of the hole. Hit down on the ball. The loft on your wedge will get the ball into the air. Trust it.

It is important that you recognize that on all of these partial swings, distance is controlled solely by the length of your backswing, not a stronger "hit" with the hands or wrists. Short shot, short backswing – longer shot, longer backswing. Rhythm should be exactly the same on every distance wedge shot, regardless of club or the length of the backswing. Strike the ball and follow through. Observe where the ball lands and how far it rolls on every practice shot. You need this constant feedback to develop feel for these shots and nail down your distances.

Don't be discouraged if your shots go wild at first. This is normal. Practicing wedge shots for distance control is a foreign exercise to most golfers – but not to good ones. Continue focusing on your target, rhythm, and the length of your backswing. Strike the ball first, and with a descending blow. If you make a divot, it must be in front (target side) of where the ball originally lay.

If you're a high handicapper, developing skill with these distance wedge shots will do more to lower your scores than anything else in this book. Be positive about learning this. Stay with it. You'll get better fast and the knowledge and skills you take away from just a few hours of practice will stay with you for the rest of your golfing days.

You won't get many shots to within eight feet of the flagstick at the start, but you will begin getting them closer than you ever did before. That will immediately translate to lower scores. You aren't seeking perfection; you're gaining experience and steadily getting better.

Once you have spent some time on these different swings, you'll be surprised at how easily you can control the distance you hit a golf ball. You'll get feedback immediately from the 50-yard shot. The next time you face a 50 or 75-yarder on the course, even if you don't put it right next to the hole, you will at least have some idea of the correct way to play the shot and you'll be able to put the ball somewhere on the putting surface and have a chance to one-putt.

Practice the same three swings with your sand wedge. If your pitching wedge goes 50 yards with the 7:30 swing, the sand wedge will probably go around 42 or 43. After that, learn the 9:00 and 10:30 swings with each wedge. Write these distances down and memorize them. It's perfectly legal to carry a notebook or tape the numbers on the shafts of the wedges so you don't have to remember them.

It's best to learn these distances when there's no wind. You also need to take temperature into account. The same swing that produces a 50-yard shot in the summertime might yield only 42 to 45 yards on a cold day.

I recommend that you use the pitching wedge whenever possible. It's easier to hit than the more lofted wedges. There will be times when you have to go over obstacles and stop the ball quickly, and you'll need the sand and lob wedges for these high shots, but use a pitching wedge any time the situation allows.

After practicing with three wedges, you'll have a known swing for nine distances (twelve, if you use the fourth wedge or a nine-iron) of less than 100 yards. You vary these distances by increasing or decreasing the length of your backswing, always using the same, steady rhythm. If your 9:00 pitching wedge swing goes 75 yards and you need to produce a distance of 70 yards, try an 8:45 swing. If you wish to hit the ball 80 yards, you can try a 9:15 swing. Experiment with the different distances and wedge swings. You will rapidly gain confidence as you begin to realize the bonanza this knowledge will mean to your game.

No golf professional can force feed you distance control skill. You must learn it by yourself. You know your own swing and you'll soon know what it feels like to make a 7:30, 9:00, or 10:30 swing. You've got to spend some time alone learning these shots, getting feedback and recording your results. There's no other way.

After only a few productive hours with the wedges, you will be able to produce a fairly accurate shot of any distance from within 100 yards of a flagstick. Know your distances, write them down or memorize them. Practice these wedge shots at least thirty minutes a week for a month or two – more if you want to improve even faster. Nothing else you do will help your game more. You're a high handicapper, so accept the fact that you're going to hit many poor shots as you determine your wedge distances. Ignore them. Don't get discouraged. This is something new and different, so hang in there. If you want to be a real golfer, this is one step you cannot skip.

I was around a twenty-one handicapper when I started using this system. As I practiced, I disregarded my bad shots and kept trying to get a feel for how far my wedge shots traveled. It didn't take long.

Resolve to keep at this until you have the knowledge you need. Even if you cannot at first be confident in these wedge shots, you'll soon know how far each one should go, and you can plan your playing strategy around that knowledge.

A high handicapper has the opportunity to play some kind of wedge shot on nearly every hole. Gain proficiency at these shots and your poor opponents will soon go broke.

Make Your Golf Dream A Reality

POINTS TO REMEMBER

- You can hit beautiful drives all day long and still shoot 120 if your short game stinks.
- 4 out of every 5 shots you hit during a round of golf demand distance control.
- The ability to control the distance one hits the ball, particularly inside of 100 yards, is the defining difference between a real golfer and a hacker.
- You must know from experience exactly how far you hit every club in your bag.
- High handicappers nearly always hit their approach shots short of the flagstick and usually short of the green itself. They often do it twice on the same hole.
- In order to score, you must be able to use your wedges with measured swings to produce any shot of 35 to 100 yards in length.
- Learn three swings (7:30, 9:00, and 10:30) with each wedge, producing three precise distances.
- Always practice with an aim club.
- For more distance, increase the length of your backswing; for less distance, decrease the length of your backswing. Use the same rhythm on every distance wedge shot.
- Trying to lift or scoop the ball is fatal. Hit DOWN on the ball. The loft of the club will get the ball into the air.
- Stay positive and ignore your bad shots when practicing short wedges.
- A high handicapper has the opportunity to play a short wedge shot on nearly every hole. Get good at these shots and you get good at golf.

8

On and Around the Green

Every golfer misses a large number of greens in regulation. High handicappers miss practically all of them. The manner in which golfers finish these holes determines whether they shoot in the 70s, 80s, 90s, or worse. Making precise chips and pitches and one-putting are hallmarks of first-rate golfers. They make par after par from these short distances. From 100 yards and in, high handicappers pile up strokes so fast it makes your head spin.

This chapter covers shots inside 35 yards. A primary fault of high handicappers attempting this type of shot is failure to get the ball to the hole on the first try. Inexperienced golfers, playing from 20 to 35 yards out, consistently leave their first shot woefully short, often not getting the ball even halfway to the flagstick, and the tragic part is that they might do it six to ten times every time they play. They waste a full stroke every time it happens. For some mysterious and unexplained reason, human beings seem to have a deep and unnatural fear of knocking a golf ball all the way to the hole.

In order to be successful on and around the green, you have to become more proficient at pitching, chipping, sand play, and putting. Again, I implore you here, stay positive. You can do this. A little practice goes a very long way. Two hours of focused practice on the shots taught in this chapter will yield wonderful results. As little as four or five serious hours of practice can make a marked difference in the 100-shooter's game and result in a significant handicap drop. I don't mean five hours at once, but perhaps five sessions of an hour each. Afterwards, when you are standing near a green with a wedge in your hand, you'll have an idea about how to play the shot successfully. You know what length backswing will get the ball to the hole, and with this knowledge, you have a chance to hole it or get it up and down. As Dennis Bowman taught me early on, "That's what golf is all about."

All of these shots require feel and distance control. Nobody can teach you feel. You can be taught the correct techniques for these shots all day long, but you have to learn to control distance on your own. You have to hit enough of these shots quietly and contemplatively to learn how far each one will travel. This is a major step in the process of becoming a real golfer. It doesn't take "hours a day." It takes only a few hours at the beginning and maybe fifteen or twenty hours a year to maintain.

The Pitch Shot

The pitch shot is a miniature version of the full swing. Pitch shots are normally high, soft landing shots, 35 yards and shorter. You'll use the pitch shot to get over bunkers, hills, bushes, water, and other obstructions around the green. Like all short shots, the goal of the pitch is to get the ball close enough to the hole to one-putt.

With the pitch shot, unlike the chip, you can rotate your body and hips as you swing. It's best to use as little wrist as possible, but at times it's necessary to use wrist action out of high grass.

On and Around the Green

When you hit pitch shots you have to accelerate through the ball. Like all short game shots, you control distance with the length of your backswing. If your backswing is too long you'll be forced to decelerate; if the backswing is too short, you'll have to get "wristy" to get the ball to the hole. To ensure a good shot, many pros recommend "matching the ends," which means making the follow-through at least as long as the backswing.

Pitch shots are just shorter versions of the "distance wedge" shots described in Chapter 7. They are designed to fly higher than chips and stop quickly on the putting surface. Make a relaxed, rhythmic swing, hit down, and let the club loft the ball and fly it high. Scooping and trying to lift the ball will only lead to trouble.

Practice

Like every other short game shot, the pitch shot requires strict distance control. Your aim should be fairly accurate from 35 yards and closer, but you have to experiment with varying backswings to learn how far you hit each wedge. Get around the practice green and try hitting five shots to within eight feet of the flagstick from 35 yards, 30 yards, 25 yards, and then 20 yards. Do this once or twice each month, paying attention to your backswings and the distances they produce. You'll quickly develop a feel for it. Use different wedges as you practice. As you get better at this, you will have a new confidence when these situations come up in actual play – and your scores will improve.

Chipping

When you miss a green in regulation, you still have an opportunity to make par with a one-putt. That's a positive way to look at the situation. Expert chippers make par after par from off the green on days when their ball striking is off. This saves five to ten shots per round over the hacker, whose first chip or pitch doesn't get halfway to the hole, leading to bogeys and double bogeys from the same situations. Keep in mind that tour professionals get up and down from off the green more than two times out of every three, and those numbers include bunker shots.

Setup and Technique

Just as with distance wedges and pitches, you have to hit your chip shots with a descending and accelerating blow. Form the image of "dragging" the ball onto the green when you chip and strike the ball before you hit the ground.

To encourage a downward strike, take a narrow stance; turn the toes of both feet thirty degrees toward the target, and position the ball well back, flush with your heels. The worse the lie, the farther back in your stance you want the ball. Next, put 65 percent of your weight on the left foot and deloft the club, making sure your hands are well in front of the club head. Grip down on the club as low as is comfortable for you. Your lower hand can even be on the shaft. The closer your hands are to the ball, the easier it is to hit precise chip shots. Finally, keep the heel of the club off the ground. This prevents fat shots. Strike the ball with a descending blow, keeping the hands ahead of the club head at all times. The chip is a product of the back and shoulder muscles, not the wrists. Keep the back of the left hand moving toward the target without breaking your wrists.

Which Club?

Different situations call for different chipping clubs. Use the club that will allow you to land the ball two to three feet onto the green and let it roll the rest of the way to the hole. This method is more reliable than trying to fly the ball all the way to the hole and stop it close. If you are near the edge of the green, you can try the "eight-iron putt" described later in this chapter. If you are farther back and have plenty of green to work with, a nine-iron may work well. When you have little green to work with, a sand or lob wedge may offer the only chance to get the ball close enough for a chance at a one-putt.

On and Around the Green

When planning your chip shot, pick a spot on the green where you want to land the ball. Allow for as much roll as possible. Choose your chipping club and landing spot on the green based on the following formula:

Club	Fly Distance	Ground Roll
Lob Wedge	3/4	1/4
Sand Wedge	2/3	1/3
Pitching Wedge	1/2	1/2
8-iron	1/3	2/3
6-iron	1/4	3/4

If the chip is uphill, take more club and use the same rhythm and swing. The same holds true going downhill. A downhill chip that would necessitate an eight-iron on level ground might require only a nine-iron or even a pitching wedge.

These numbers all assume that you have some green to work with. You often hear the term "short sided." This means that the approach shot has left very little green between the ball and the flagstick and requires a lofted shot to the green. Lofted shots are far more difficult than chips where there's plenty of green to work with. Short siding yourself typically costs at least one extra shot. Be conservative and aim your longer approach shots at the middle of the green.

To review: Let the big muscles of the back and shoulders do the work on chip shots. Grip low on the club and keep the hands ahead of the club face. Relax, pick the right club and the correct landing spot for that club. Let your arms and wrists feel soft, make a smooth, slow backswing, and then accelerate through the ball, hands in front, holding the club only tightly enough with the left hand to prevent it from twisting when it makes contact with the ball.

Practice

Once you've decided on your chipping clubs, you'll have to spend some time practicing in order to know how far each stroke sends the ball. It's easy to hit the right line with a chip if you pick a target spot just in front of the ball. Distance control is the difficult part, and it is different for each chipping club. Most golfers don't like chipping practice, but the following drill will make it interesting, and at the same time allow you to measure your progress.

The Seven-Ball Drill

Chipping greens are usually empty, so while other players are busy working on "the swing," you can be improving your golf scores with this drill.

Grab your wedges and the six, eight, and nine-irons. Next, drop seven balls around the green, creating shots that you would hit with a pitching wedge. Move around the green, chipping each ball to the hole. When you are finished, remove the three worst and the three best chips. Measure and record (in feet) the distance of the remaining ball from the hole. That represents your median distance. Next, switch clubs, set up different shots and do the drill again. Record your median distance with the new club.

It doesn't take long to do the drill three or four times with different clubs. Use your imagination and hit from every kind of lie – uphill, side hill and downhill, good and bad lies. You'll be surprised how quickly your median distance improves. Once you learn to get a lot of these shots inside five feet, your scores will take another jump downward. Don't spend hours doing this. Just do the drill occasionally and stay positive. It will help you develop and retain "feel," and the benefits are incalculable.

The Eight-Iron "Putt."

You've missed the green with your approach shot, but your ball is only three or four feet from the edge. You have plenty of green to work with, but the grass around your ball is too heavy for a putter. What's the right shot? The eight-iron putt.

The pro who taught it to me said it was so easy it seemed like cheating, and he was right. Set up in your normal putting stance, but with your eight-iron instead of the putter. Grip down on the shaft and keep a little extra weight on your left side. Put the ball about an inch back in your stance. Keeping the heel of the club off the ground, use your normal putting stroke.

The shot is simple and will give you great results, but you must practice before using it in actual play. When I started using this shot, my tendency was to hit the ball too far. Now, I pretend I am putting and just hit with a little less power. The shot lofts the ball over the fringe grass, lands it on the green, and scoots it to the hole, just like a putt. It is much easier than hitting a wedge from this distance. Give this shot one practice session of 45 minutes. Learn it from varying distances around the green and you instantly have an important scoring weapon you'll be able to use for the rest of your life.

The "Texas Wedge" (Putting from off the green)

Anytime you can putt a ball from off the green, do it. Lofting a golf ball is always more dangerous than rolling it. When the grass is matted low in the winter, I am sometimes able to putt from 20 yards off the green. I can always get a putt closer than a pitch or chip.

Putting

As I was finishing this book, Dennis Bowman described an entirely different method of putting he'd recently learned about. Of course, I was interested, so Dennis spent fifteen minutes teaching it to me. I walked away with a potent new weapon and a load of confidence.

Dennis told me that recent computer studies have revealed that the very best putters who ever lived use a stroke that hardly anybody teaches today.

Make Your Golf Dream A Reality

Most of us learned either the "straight back and straight through" putting stroke, or the "inside to inside" stroke. But the best putters of all time haven't used either of these methods.

Brilliant putters like Bobby Locke, Tiger Woods, and Ben Crenshaw appear to use a slight *inside to outside* stroke and putt the ball with a little *draw*. I can't prove this and I know you are gasping in disbelief, particularly if you're an instructor, but at least hear me out.

From about eight feet, Dennis made a chalk line straight to the middle of the hole. He then put down a line about a foot long at the point I was putting from. This short line crossed the line to the hole and was angled very slightly (about three degrees) from inside to out. I placed my ball at the point the lines intersected. Dennis then said to keep my putter aimed at the hole and to swing along the inside-to-outside path line. The final ingredient, he told me, was to add loft to the putter before I started the backstroke.

I set up in my normal stance, aligned the putter face with the longer line to the hole, added loft by moving my hands about an inch to the right and, keeping my aim at the hole, stroked the putter along the shorter "inside to out" line. The solid sound and feel of contact with the ball was wonderfully different from my usual stroke. I putted ball after ball, short putts and long, with an entirely new feel to my putting. I didn't make every putt, but they all made it to the hole, and they rolled with more authority than putts with my old stroke. I immediately adopted the new method and it has served me well.

These are the steps:
1. Align the putter face directly down your target line.
2. Add loft to the putter by moving your hands slightly to the right.
3. Start the putter back to the inside and release it to the outside.

If you're a good putter and happy with your putting, don't fix what's not broken. If your stroke needs some help, however, try this method. It might bring new life into your putting.

On and Around the Green

****

Speed is more important than line on longer putts. On putts ranging from twenty to forty feet, hitting a faulty line shouldn't leave a second putt of more than three or four feet. But if speed is incorrect, you can be looking at six to ten feet. Learn speed and you'll seldom three-putt. Distance control rules on the greens, just like on the course.

Keep track of the number of putts you take per eighteen-hole round. For record-keeping purposes, a putt is defined as any shot you hit from the actual putting surface. If you use the "Texas Wedge," record the stroke as a chip. That's how they score it on the tours, and you should do the same.

You hope that the number of putts you record in eighteen holes of golf will never exceed 36. To score in the 70s, you will usually take no more than 32.

Putting is the simplest of the golf strokes, and there are a hundred different styles. It requires very little strength, so anyone can do it. Be positive, read the break, commit to the line, have a set routine, and finally, moving nothing but your arms and shoulders, make a confident stroke and roll the ball into the hole. It sounds simple, but these steps are the very foundation for good putting.

The Putting Grip

As long as the grip you are using allows you to square the putter as you stroke the putt, there's no reason to change it. There are as many different grips as there are golfers. I would only suggest that you keep your grip pressure as light as possible while keeping control of the putter. Control means that if you hit the ball slightly toward the heel or toe of the putter, it won't twist in your hands and start the putt off line.

Rhythm

Use the same rhythm on every putt. Count "one" on the backstroke and "two" on the follow-through. Let the club swing the same distance back and forward, always accelerating through the ball. Keep the same rhythm for both short and long putts, changing only the length of your backswing to increase or decrease the distance the putt travels. When you fear putting past the hole, it's easy to stop the putter just as you make contact with the ball. Keep your backswing short enough to allow the putter to accelerate and release through.

Feel for Distance

Good lag putting eliminates three-putts and saves strokes. Just as with chipping and pitching, no one can teach you distance control and feel. You have to learn it from experience. Spend a few minutes on the practice green before each round, practicing fifteen, twenty, twenty-five, and thirty-footers. This gives you a feel for the conditions you will face when you begin play.

A good way to learn distance control on the green is to place a ball twenty feet away and putt another ball three feet past it. Putt another ball three feet past that one, continuing in three-foot increments until you reach about forty feet. Next, try to come back, starting at forty feet, putting each ball three feet shorter than the previous one until you are back to about twenty feet. Use the same rhythm always, with longer or shorter backswings controlling the distance. Spend fifteen minutes a week for three weeks on this drill and watch your lag putting improve.

The putter head must be accelerating when it strokes the ball. Short putts need only a small backswing; longer putts, longer backswings. If you have a three-footer and take a big backswing, you will be forced to decelerate as the putter approaches the ball. Take a shorter backswing on these short putts and confidently knock them in with a rhythmic, accelerating stroke.

Call It a "Tap-In."

My friend and golf teacher, Bob Love, of Fairfield Bay, Arkansas, is an amazing putter. Bob taught me what I call the "tap-in" drill. It's simple, and it helps put you in the right frame of mind before you putt. Bob takes four or five golf balls and drops them in a circle three or four feet around the hole. He then starts talking and putting. He approaches a ball and says, "It's just a little tap-in," and strokes it in the hole. Without wasting any time, he walks to the next ball, sets up, and repeats, "It's just a little tap-in" and he knocks that one in.

When he's made them all from short range, he moves back to six or seven feet and repeats the procedure. Then, he goes to nine or ten feet and does it again. I've watched Bob make an entire circle of balls from about ten feet without missing. It's an amazing sight to behold. He doesn't give himself time to start worrying. He just looks at the putt, calls it a tap-in, and strokes it in the hole.

Most of us do the exact opposite. We face a ten-footer and tell ourselves there's hardly any chance we'll make it, or it's going to break more than we think. We start worrying about the consequences of a three-putt or a new bet. By the time we actually hit the ball, we're tied up in knots. Calling the putt a "tap-in" immediately takes the pressure off. Our minds have been conditioned to expect that we'll hole every tap-in, and this promotes confidence.

Confidence is your most valuable asset when you putt. Bobby Locke, one of the best putters of all time, put it this way: "Approaching a putt with doubt in your mind is nearly always fatal." So, remember the days of confidence, those days when the hole looked as big as a trash can and your confidence soared. You felt as if you'd make the putt even before you stroked it. Hold onto that positive attitude when you see a makable putt before you and say to yourself, "It's just a little tap-in."

Routine

Your conscious mind prepares you for the putt (green reading, judging wind, grain and moisture, etc.), but as you start the putter back, you should be on automatic pilot. Let the putt happen instead of trying to force matters. This feeling of "autopilot" comes from following the same routine again and again.

Alignment

Just as in the full swing, your mind can play tricks on you. What feels like correct putting alignment is often way off the mark. Have a friend help line your feet and shoulders parallel to the target line. Your eyes should be directly over the ball. Keep your feet at shoulder width. You need a solid base, as there is a tendency to sway if the feet are too close together.

Stay *Perfectly* Still

The most common cause of missed short putts is peeking. The golfer anxiously tries to see if the ball goes into the hole. Peekers move their head and shoulders as they stroke the ball. This tends to throw the putter head off line and results in a missed putt. The remedy is simple – keep your head and body absolutely still when you make the stroke. Focus on a dimple on the back of the ball and move only the arms and shoulders as you stroke it. Keep the back of your left hand moving straight down the target line and don't move your head. On short putts, listen for the sound of the ball as it falls into the hole. Try it. You'll be surprised and pleased with the results.

Go back and re-read pages 33 and 34 of this book to review how I've successfully overcome short putt troubles.

Green Reading

Green reading skill comes with experience. If you play the same golf course often, you have a good idea how the greens break. Wind, length of the grass, temperature, and moisture are among the endless variety of factors that make putting different every day, even on the same course.

As you approach a green, particularly on a strange course, ask yourself the question, "How would water drain off this green?" Take a quick look at the line your ball will travel and remember your first impression. Your first subconscious impression is probably very close to correct. Without stepping on anybody's line, walk as close as possible along the line your ball must travel, letting your feet feel slopes that might be hard to see.

The best information you can receive about the speed and break of your putt comes from watching your playing partners' putts. If you are lucky, another player's ball will travel on a line close to yours. Pay close attention. Play more break on fast greens than on slow greens. Amateurs' putts pass below the hole 85 percent of the time on breaking putts, never having had a chance to go in. Form the habit of playing more break than you think, and visualize your ball going in on the high side of the hole. That way, you'll have a chance to make it.

Aim Past the Hole

Many golfers are too timid with the putter. The dread of three-putting leads to lags on putts that you should be trying to hole. Try to hit the putt a foot to a foot and a half past the hole. That guarantees enough speed to hold the line, but if you miss, it leaves an easy comeback putt.

No Wrist

Putting is a function of the big muscles. You may need to use some wrist action on putts of 30 feet or more, but putts shorter than that should be propelled by the big muscles of the back and shoulders. Don't overdo the backswing, and stroke the ball smoothly with acceleration.

Make the Five-Footer Your Best Friend

I heard an interesting story about a team of college golfers at Oral Roberts University in Tulsa, Oklahoma. Their coach gave them a task to complete every day before they were allowed on the course. Each player had to make ten consecutive three-footers, then ten consecutive four-footers, and finally ten consecutive five-footers. If the player missed at any point, he had to start over at putt number one (for that length). This drill could take some golfers all week long, but these were good players, and it made great short putters of them all.

Try a modified version. Make five in a row from three feet, four feet, and then five feet. If you miss, start over. You'll feel pressure on that fifth putt. Don't hit the same putt over and over. Place your golf balls around the hole.

Five in a row will be difficult from five feet, but if you do this exercise a few times each month, over time you will make hundreds and eventually thousands of these short putts. Your brain will record all of these "makes." You'll also form the habit of getting the ball to the hole. You won't be so afraid of lag putting, because you'll have confidence you can make the three or four-footer, even if you've hit a bad first putt. Watch the tour pros on TV. They smack those short putts into the back of the hole without a second thought. Try the system I described on page 34. On putts five feet and shorter, read the putt, line it up, take a couple of practice strokes, and look at the hole as you make the stroke. This system still works well for me.

Bear in mind that all putts are really straight. When you have a breaking putt, pick a spot on your target line and hit a straight putt to an imaginary hole on that line.

Sand Play

High handicappers are more terrified and discouraged by sand than anything else on the golf course. This fear is justified. I have hit more embarrassing and stupid-looking shots from the sand than all other types combined. For a long time I feared the sand. I would hit into a greenside bunker and automatically think to myself, "double bogey." That attitude didn't help matters.

Weak golfers always seem to have trouble from the sand. Sand naturally makes them nervous after having experienced repeated failures to extract the ball from the bunker or skulling rocket balls in every direction. This leads to a tightening of the muscles, fear, and negative thoughts. The poor golfer has no chance.

We've all learned the standard greenside bunker "explosion" shot. To review, aim your feet left of the target and aim (open) the club face to the target. Weaken your left hand grip (turn it to the left on the grip) and hit the sand an inch and a half to two inches behind the ball. Follow through, keeping everything except your arms perfectly still. From normal lies, put the ball forward in your stance and make sure to place more weight on your left side. This system works, but like all golf shots, it takes a little practice to get good at it. Mark Maness, a Dallas professional, instructed me to keep the grip of my club pointed straight up when I set up for sand shots. I had, without realizing it, developed the bad habit of delofting my wedge before I swung. My bunker play immediately improved.

The most helpful tip I can give you about sand play is simply to watch the tour pros on TV. It is amazing to see how relaxed and smoothly they make their backswings and follow through. After watching a tour event on television one day in 2004, I went to the course, played a few holes, and then stepped into a bunker to practice. I tried to imitate the sand shots I had just seen on television. I set up my normal way and told myself to relax my body, particularly the arms. I then made a s-l-o-w, relaxed backswing, and accelerated through the ball, just like I had seen the pros do. I came down softly into the sand behind the ball and followed through in the same, relaxed manner that I saw on TV. The ball zipped perfectly out of the sand, landed softly, and rolled to within seven feet of the flagstick, about thirty-five feet away.

Again and again, I kept relaxing and hitting the sand smoothly and slowly. I was perhaps applying the speed and intensity of hitting a 30-yard sand wedge off a fairway lie. I practiced hitting different distances by simply increasing or decreasing the length of my backswing, always trying to keep the same tempo. This method yielded the best sand session in my life. Sand practice is something I do on a regular basis. I don't spend a lot of time on it, 10-15 minutes at a time, totaling maybe four hours a year, but these brush-up sessions keep my confidence up.

If you've never been shown the basics of sand play, you need to take a bunker lesson from your pro. Once you have the method, r-e-l-a-x everything before you make that smooth sand shot – and practice it once in a while.

If you're a mid or high handicapper, make it your primary goal to get somewhere on the green with your sand shots. A two-putt will usually yield a bogey, and that's sufficient at the start. After you get some practice at these shots, you can work on controlling distance and start getting some of them up and down.

POINTS TO REMEMBER

- Every golfer has numerous chances to get up and down for par from off the green.
- The pitch shot is a miniature version of the full swing.
- The goal of the chip or pitch shot is to get the ball into one-putt range.
- Whether you're putting, chipping, or pitching, stay down and accelerate through the ball.
- In an eighteen-hole round of golf, a skilled chipper can turn five to seven probable bogeys into pars.
- Chip with different clubs in varying situations.
- Keep your hands in front of the club head when you chip.
- To chip, use the muscles of the back and shoulders, not the wrists.
- Practice chipping with the seven-ball drill to learn distance control and "feel."
- Use the "eight-iron putt" when you are within five feet of the green.
- Use the "Texas wedge" whenever possible.
- Try the "inside to outside" draw putt. It's the stroke used by the best putters of all time.
- The speed of a putt is four times more important than line.
- Keep track of your putts per round. To score in the 70s, you should average no more than 30-32 putts per eighteen holes.
- Putting is the simplest of the golf strokes. It requires very little strength, so anybody can learn to putt well.
- Use the same rhythm for both short and long putts, varying only the length of your backswing to control distance.
- Confidence is an essential ingredient to good putting.
- When you putt, align your feet and shoulders parallel to the target line.
- Keep your head and body perfectly still when you putt.
- Make the five-foot putt your best friend.

On and Around the Green

- Learn the basics of the greenside sand explosion shot.
- Point the shaft of the club straight up when you hit from the sand (don't deloft it).
- Watch the PGA pros hit sand shots and imitate their rhythm.
- When you hit from the sand, r-e-l-a-x, swing smoothly, and follow through.
- A high handicap golfer can make noteworthy progress by devoting five hours to the shots described in this chapter.

9

Play Within Yourself

You've sliced your drive into the trees. It's a par four and you can reach the green with a career four-iron if you keep it low and get the ball between the trunks of two oak trees 30 yards ahead. You also have the option to play safe by chipping out to the fairway, leaving yourself a seven- or eight-iron to the green.

"What the heck?" you think as you tensely yank out the four-iron. The ball bangs hard into a tree and flies straight out-of-bounds. You sheepishly take a drop, chip out to the fairway, and card a seven or eight instead of the bogey five you would probably have made chipping out in the first place. High handicappers constantly make these high risk and score-killing decisions.

The same can be said for charging putts. You must ask yourself if it's worth the risk of knocking your ball five or six feet past the hole. Depending on the circumstances, it may occasionally be worth it, but you'll usually turn in lower scores by playing conservatively. Tommy Armour put it nicely. His advice was to play each shot so as to make the next one easy.

We watch the men and women on the pro tours make miraculous saves from seemingly impossible situations and unwisely try to do the same. These pros are the best golfers in the world and they routinely perform miracles on the golf course. Amateurs need to understand their own limitations and play accordingly.

If you have played much golf, you should have a pretty good idea of your capabilities with every club in the bag. If you stand over a shot and feel squeamish about your chances, you're probably trying for too much. If the shot would require the very best swing you ever made with the club in your hand, it's a bad idea. Chip out, lay-up, and make the next shot easy. You'll probably make bogey, but you take double bogey and worse out of the equation.

Classic high handicapper mistakes:
1. Hitting a lay-up shot to a hazard into the hazard itself.
2. Unwillingness to chip out to the fairway when it's the right choice.
3. Smashing a fairway wood its maximum distance in an attempt to reach a distant green with water, out-of-bounds, and bunkers in play.
4. Trying to hit a long shot over water to a green just on the other side.
5. Attempting a heroic, but low percentage shot from a hazard when a lay-up or drop would be far more sensible.
6. Charging putts over twenty feet. The chance of holing these putts is small and the risk of three-putting high.
7. Shooting at sucker pins, with the risks of sand, water, and getting short-sided.

The penalty for failure in these 'heroic' attempts can be as much as three or four shots, immediately destroying the round. A one-stroke bailout will normally get you back into play. If you believe your chance of making a successful shot in a precarious situation is less than 50-50, don't do it.

Match play and team events are different. If it is apparent that you are going to lose a hole playing conservatively, you can take risks that you wouldn't consider in normal stroke play.

You're not a pro. Shoot for the middle of the green, lag longer putts, chip out, lay up, and stay well clear of OBs and hazards. Attempt shots you are reasonably sure you can pull off. Play within your abilities. You'll shoot lower scores in the long run.

POINTS TO REMEMBER

- High handicappers habitually try for too much.
- You will score better playing conservatively.
- Remember Tommy Armour's advice: "Play to make the next shot easy."
- Play within your abilities.

10

No Fear

Golfers have a lot to fear: missing the fairway or green; hitting into the sand, water, trees, or out of bounds; chunking, skulling, or drop kicking; the yips; misreading putts; three-putting; not getting out of the bunker or high grass; bogey, double-bogey, or worse; being short, long, left, or right; not breaking 100, 90, 80, or 70; looking stupid; bad luck; losing their ball; being outdriven; their opponent holing out; losing bets; fear of this club or that; bad shots continuing all day; fear of failure and fear of success . . . on and on it goes.

Fear and tension are a golfer's worst enemies and fear runs thick and fast on every golf course in the world. Fears feed on each other, multiplying and inflicting untold agony on the golfer. And the poor soul is only trying to knock a white ball into a little hole.

The better you become at golf, the more important your thinking becomes. At the PGA tour level, golf is mostly mental. For many years, Tiger Woods has been the world's best golfer because in addition to his great talent and training, he knows how to control his thinking. In situations that terrify other tour players, Tiger seems to summon the courage it takes to calmly make shots that seem impossible. It's uncanny how many times he's done this on the back nine on Sunday afternoon with a tournament on the line. It's this confidence and seeming fearlessness that has separated Woods from the rest of the field.

Whether you aspire to be a scratch golfer or a single-digit handicapper, you first need to be able to see yourself achieving the goal you have chosen. With this picture firmly fixed in your mind, it is easy to get truly committed and begin developing your game. Commitment will see you through the many fears and disheartening setbacks you are bound to experience along the way.

Courage is the opposite of fear. The next time you stand anxiously over a four-foot putt, relax and tell yourself, "I have the courage and the skill to hole this putt." Notice how differently you feel when you have this belief or even attempt to have this belief. Now revert back to your old way of thinking about a four-footer. "If I miss this short putt, I'll look stupid, lose the hole, and add one more unnecessary stroke to my score."

With these thoughts swirling in your brain, your hands and arms tighten. You are likely to move your head and body as you anxiously try to peek at the result of a nervous jab. You're unable to release the putter and make a good stroke. You miss the putt, rake the ball back, and now, at last in a relaxed state, you take a deep breath, make a smooth stroke, and the ball easily falls into the heart of the hole. It's so easy to make putts when they don't count. You have no fear of missing and there's no downside. You can concentrate on holing the putt instead of what it will mean if you miss. Without the fear of failure, you are relaxed and don't really care. Imagine your golf game if you could maintain that attitude all the time.

I'll never forget an interesting tale I heard about PGA tour player Brad Faxon, one of world's best putters. Faxon was purportedly observed strolling around a practice green, putting here and there, but missing everything. When somebody finally asked him what he was doing, Faxon replied, "I'm practicing not caring if I miss." I don't know if the story is true, but it makes a good point: if you can keep from caring too much, you'll keep fear at a minimum and play better.

The same fears apply to the long game. How many times have you stood at the edge of a lake with a long carry and could think of nothing but your ball landing in the water? Or stood in a bunker in fear of not getting out?

It isn't easy for you, me, or anyone else to clear the mind of fear and think only of where we want the ball to go. But if you choose to hit shots within your capabilities, and focus on the *process* instead of result, you will not only improve, but your mis-hit shots will be far less distressing.

A fixed routine will help you overcome fear. If you choose the right shot, pick a target, go through your normal routine and aim correctly, consider the shot a success, regardless of the result. Practice this at the range, and you will likely be able to duplicate it in pressure situations on the course. If you practice without picking a target and without going through your routine, pressure shots on the course will present you with an unfamiliar feeling and allow fear to creep in.

When you're faced with a tough shot, play within your capabilities. You *should* be afraid of a shot that you only have a one-in-five chance of pulling off successfully. You're an amateur and you don't have the same arsenal of shots as the pros. Don't be too aggressive. Sacrifice one stroke to save two or three. Smart course management and playing within your capabilities help keep fear to a minimum. As a high handicapper, your primary job is to take the big number out of play. Taking needless chances leads to tension-filled golf and blowup holes.

Focus on your routine and *process* rather than results, and you'll find that in this mode of diminished fear, you'll play better. This leads to a more relaxed, less self-critical style of play and more enjoyment for you and your playing partners.

Tell yourself to have courage when you face a difficult golf situation. You don't die from hitting the ball out of bounds or into a water hazard. Keep things in perspective. Pick the appropriate shot for your skill level and pre-accept anything that might happen before you take the shot. Then you can relax, concentrate on your target, and calmly go through your routine. With this accepting attitude, you have reduced fear and greatly improved your chances of making a successful shot.

POINTS TO REMEMBER

- Golfers have many fears.
- Tension and fear are the golfer's worst enemies.
- The better you get at golf, the more important the mental aspect of the game becomes.
- A fixed routine goes a long way toward reducing fear.
- Think PROCESS rather than results.
- Dangerous shots cause fear. Play conservatively.
- Tell yourself to have courage when faced with a precarious shot.
- Pre-accept anything bad that might occur before you hit the shot. In this accepting frame of mind, you can relax, go through your routine, and give yourself the best chance of executing a successful shot.

11

Toughing It Out

"Golf is good for the soul. You get so mad at yourself you forget to hate your enemies." I concur with this quote from my fellow Oklahoman, Will Rogers. Golf sometimes makes me madder than hell. "I'm quitting golf" was always my tongue-in-cheek comment after a seemingly hopeless round. I was joking, but those feelings of frustration and helplessness can be overwhelming when the wheels come off and you shoot a dozen or more shots above your handicap.

Although low scoring is the ultimate object of golf, outside factors can produce a high number when you really haven't played badly. Play a familiar and perfectly manicured 6100-yard course on a warm and windless day, and odds are you'll shoot a good score and feel like a real golfer. Take the exact same skill level and play a 6600-yard unfamiliar, not so well-manicured course on a cold and windy day and you're likely to shoot a dozen shots higher and be ready to give the game up. Your skill level remained the same. Only the environment changed. Even so, after a bad day, there's a tendency to feel like all your practice time has been wasted and you're back to square one.

On August 26, 2000, my handicap was at thirteen. I shot a 76 at Sequoyah State Park that day, my first time ever to break 80. It was a fantastic day, but a closer look at my posted scores shows that this landmark round was preceded by six straight rounds above my handicap and was followed by a 22 over par 94. But I remember August of 2000 as a happy time, and only because of that round.

If you want to feel better when you're slumping, take a look at the PGA tour leaderboard after the Friday round. Check below the cut line and find the players who packed up and went home empty handed. You'll see major champions, multiple tour winners, and guys who might have won the previous week or two. Not even the world's best golfers are immune to bad rounds, struggle, and discouragement. They just handle it better than most 25-handicappers.

It's productive to have high expectations for the long term, but not for a single round or tournament. You have to hang in there and keep the improvement process going, no matter how discouraged you get. Occasionally, you just have a bad day, but if you play badly for several rounds in a row, find the problem and take care of it.

David Leadbetter's *Faults and Fixes—How to Correct the 80 Most Common Problems in Golf* has pulled me from the quicksand more times than I care to count. Every golfer should have his own copy of this informative book. Be resourceful. Do whatever you have to do to get your game back on track.

If you play a lot, a good fix can be doing nothing. Too much golf causes staleness and boredom, leading to a slump. A short layoff can dissolve your troubles. View golf improvement as a long-term project. You can make incredible progress in a season or two, but expect spells of struggle and disappointment along the way. They are simply aspects of the game that come and go for every golfer.

You can't guess when amazing and unforgettable events might occur on the golf course. Your best round ever could be tomorrow, your next par three might yield a hole-in-one, your next par five, an eagle. Every golf shot is unique and independent and you have but one chance to make the most of it. Put it in this perspective – you are going to hit a finite number of golf shots in your lifetime. Every shot you take leaves you with one fewer. Decide how you want to treat the shots remaining in your inventory.

Throw off discouragement and continue working to overcome the weaknesses that are keeping you from shooting in the 70s. Learn to set up and aim. Play from the right tees. Get some reliable distance control shots from short range. Use impact tape and swing aids to improve your ball striking. Take a lesson when you're stymied. These measures will pay huge dividends in the long run, and that's where you need to be looking.

Television coverage of golf can be misleading. Cameras stay on tournament leaders and their closest chasers. We become accustomed to seeing tour pros on their very best days. If the leader has a bad hole or two and slips back in the pack, the cameras drop him or her and dash to the hot new leader. We know that great golfers have bad rounds, too, but we don't get to experience the struggle with them. The player of the hour must always be front and center. Watching tour pros every week can lead to the false impression that it's possible to play flawless golf day after day and our expectations become warped.

****

This book doesn't contain the standard "mental game" chapter. My purpose is to coach high handicappers on the nuts and bolts of golf and get them shooting below 80 as quickly as possible. First, they have to get good equipment, move to the right tees, and learn how to set up and aim straight. The next step is learning to control distance with wedges and improving their pitching and chipping. Those steps, coupled with a mentality that does not give up in the face of discouragement can quickly produce a real golfer.

For mental game training, high handicappers can profit from two outstanding books by Dr. Robert Rotella: *Golf Is Not a Game of Perfect*, and *Golf Is a Game of Confidence.* I read these books during my first year of golf and I highly recommend them both.

POINTS TO REMEMBER

- Outside factors can produce a high score when you haven't played badly.
- If you want to feel better when you're slumping, take a look at the PGA tour leaderboard after the Friday (cut) round.
- You are going to hit a finite number of golf shots in your lifetime. Every shot you take leaves you with one fewer. Be good to your remaining inventory.
- Struggle and disappointment are aspects of golf that come and go for everyone.
- Overcome discouragement and continue working on the basics outlined in this book, week by week and month by month.

12

Safe and Simple

This chapter presents more practical ideas to help knock strokes off your game. As a high handicapper, you've got to constantly be aware of and manage anything that's adding shots to your scores. Simply taking a swing lesson now and then won't do the job. "Hitting balls" without picking a target and setting up correctly won't help either and only ingrains bad habits.

Think. Analyze your game. Be aware of what's costing you strokes. Make the most of your practice time. When you practice, pick a target and go through your routine on every shot. When you get into trouble on the course, don't risk triple bogey trying to force a doubtful par. Take your bogey and move on. Be smart and play conservatively. You have to learn to reduce blowup holes.

Keep a record of fairways and greens hit and count your putts. One-putts are your best friends. When you start making five to eight one-putts per round, you'll know your short game is on track. One-putts are as much an indicator of good pitching and chipping as of putting itself.

Tee off on the same side as the trouble. If there is a lake running down the right side of the fairway, hit from the right side of the tee box. That keeps your aim away from the hazard.

If a par three green is enveloped with high rough, water, bunkers, or other hazards, consider laying up to a safe area. There's usually such a spot 10 or 15 yards short of the green. From there, you can employ your improving short game skills to pitch or chip the ball close to the hole and make a one-putt par. Even if you have to settle for bogey, you've avoided the blowup. You can play any treacherous approach shot in the same manner. Don't be afraid of accepting bogey on these difficult holes. You'll make more pars and birdies as your short game continues to get better.

Lay up well short of cross-fairway hazards. Even if you can't reach the green on your next shot, the short game will keep par in play. A ball hit into a water hazard almost always results in double bogey or worse.

Play safely from greenside bunkers. If there's a high lip in front or another hazard is on the opposite side of the green, consider hitting out sideways. You might sacrifice a stroke, but you take the possibility of the big blowup out of the picture.

Be constantly aware of wind speed and direction. Recognize the difference between a one-club wind and a two or three-club wind. Understand that a high shot into the wind can balloon and travel half of its normal distance. Learn to hit low punch shots and learn how to control distance on these shots (ball back in stance, delofted club face, and shorter follow-through).

If you're inclined to experiment, try playing a reckless eighteen-hole round, shooting for every pin, regardless of danger or distance. Be daring – cut corners, ignore hazards, high grass, bunkers, and out-of-bounds markers. Putt boldly and try to hole everything, regardless of length. Throw all caution to the wind. After that, play another eighteen holes doing the very opposite. Play conservatively. Lay up. Chip out from trouble. Be willing to make bogey, but take no chances on blowup holes. Shoot for the middle of the green. Avoid short siding yourself. Lag longer putts to a three-foot circle. Respect every hazard. Compare scorecards when you're done. The conservative round will almost always yield a lower score. Maybe you made fewer pars, but you reduced blowup holes to a minimum. That's the high handicapper's first job.

It all boils down to Tommy Armour's outstanding advice: "Play to make the next shot easy."

POINTS TO REMEMBER

- Be aware of and manage anything that's adding shots to your scores.
- Keep close track of your one-putts. When you start making five to eight one-putts per round, you'll know your short game is on track.
- Lay up short in treacherous approach situations.
- Be aware of the wind.
- Play conservatively.
- Play to make the next shot easy.

13

Now Do It!

By now, I hope you have decided what you want from the game of golf. You're not trying to win the U.S. Open or get on the tour. You simply want to shave enough strokes from your scorecard to become a happy golfer – and hopefully reach single digits.

You've learned that the easiest methods of reducing strokes are: 1) using good equipment, 2) playing from the right tees, 3) learning to set up and aim straight 4) controlling distance, particularly from short range, and 5) playing to make the next shot easy. You understand that the one-putt is your best friend and you have to learn to get your pitches and chips all the way to the hole on the first attempt.

Regardless of what you might think today, distance control and short game practice is fun, rewarding, and addictive. Getting good at short shots won't take nearly as much time and effort as you believe.

If you're still thinking, "I'll learn distance control and short shots someday later, after I get my swing down," you haven't been paying attention. It works the other way around. Learning to hit shorter shots successfully leads to better ball striking and better full shots. If you cannot accept the importance of accurate short shots with distance control, resign yourself to mediocre golf. You'll go to your grave with a high handicap.

Just a few hours of thoughtful and resolute effort on distance control wedges, pitching, and chipping can transform any high handicapper's game. Resolve to make the start now. Stay with it during the tough times. Don't ever let a month go by without some distance control wedge, pitching, and chipping practice. Not hours a day – just two or three serious hours a month. The reward for this modest amount of practice is worth a hundred times the effort expended.

****

The remainder of this chapter contains ideas for action that will propel you to your handicap goal. To quickly review important training exercises and suggestions in this book, refer back to the **Points to Remember** summaries at the end of each chapter.

Golfers often forget important principles. In order to keep your thinking sharp on the course, I have included a page of reminders to scan just before practice or play. Make a copy and read it before you head to the course.

Keep your thoughts on the *benefits* headed your way. Picture a healthy scorecard showing scores ten to twenty strokes better than you shoot today. Get better at the long game with the suggestions in Chapter 6. Imagine the strokes you will save when you can count on getting your ball on the green from the 100-yard range and closer. Imagine getting your pitch and chip shots all the way to the hole on the first attempt. Think of all the one-putts and par saves that will replace double and triple bogeys as you develop your distance control, chipping and pitching skills.

Many swing problems are the result of setup and aim errors. Your long game eventually needs to be good enough to get you on six to nine greens in regulation. You have to be playing the right tees to have a chance to achieve that.

When you do miss greens, a good short game will still earn you plenty of pars and keep the big numbers off your scorecard. The secret is always distance control. No professional can give or teach you distance control skill. You have to learn it on your own. You have no other choice if you want to be a real golfer.

The time you spend learning and expanding your ability to hit new shots and distances brings you ever closer to your ultimate goal and hopefully a single-digit handicap or better. As little as half an hour of practice can teach you one valuable distance control shot – and you have it forever. Every new shot you learn can be immediately incorporated into your game to help start lowering your scores.

Continue increasing the number of shots you can reasonably expect to carry out successfully. Week by week, month by month, and season by season, your game will gain strength. As you add to the shots you can successfully execute, they'll become like old friends, always ready to help place your ball safely on the green. Whenever you approach your golf ball, you'll have a specific club and known swing to place the ball close to the hole. That's what golf is all about.

The Short Game Handicap Test

The short game handicap test provides a sure-fire method for gauging your progress. I suggest you take the test every two or three months. Keep a record of your results and compare them with your previous tests. Your weaknesses will be exposed, as plain as day.

Dave Pelz provides a short game handicap test and scoring system in *Dave Pelz's Short Game Bible*. The test is a great idea, but I believe the scoring standard for Pelz's test is too difficult for higher handicappers. No shot landing outside six feet scores even a point. It's easy to score poorly, become discouraged, and give up.

For readers of this book, I've put together a friendlier short game handicap test. It first rewards shots good enough to get a ball on the green, and it highly rewards shots that could lead to a one-putt – within the magical eight-foot circle around the hole. Take the test as soon as you finish reading the book and repeat it four to six times a year. Get a friend to take the test with you. Competition makes for fun and tension, similar to actual play. The handicap test is itself a superb short game practice session.

Instructions for playing these shots can be found in Chapters 7 and 8. Use the setup and swing methods taught in those chapters. Pick a ground target in front of your ball before every shot and line up everything with that spot. Always keep in mind that you are practicing *distance control.* Distance control is the real secret of golf, and you learn it only through experience, but you learn it fast.

After you complete each test, record your score. Then clear the balls from the green and move to the next test. To best judge your progress, use the same practice area every time you test. If possible, take the test on level ground and give yourself some green to work with. You are learning to hit the ball precise distances. For the purpose of determining these distances, it's best to take odd bounces out of play.

If you have plenty of practice time, take the short game handicap test every week or so. It takes less than an hour using five balls per test. It's fun, and you won't find a faster way to get good at the short game.

The Short Game Handicap Test

Test one. Set up 100 yards from the target. Hit your most reliable 100-yard shot. This is the most difficult test, so don't get discouraged if you don't score well. Depending on your strength and age, you might use anything from a pitching wedge to a six-iron. Use a pitching wedge wherever possible, unless the test asks for a different club or you can't reach the green with the suggested club. Hit five shots on each test (ten if you have plenty of time). Tally your results based on each ball's distance from the hole. Score no points for balls hit outside the maximum distance listed for each test, for example, 30 feet in test one.

8-30 feet = 1 point
Inside 8 feet= 4 points
Hole out = 6 points

Test two. Set up 75 yards from your target. Pitching wedge.
8-25 feet = 1 point
Inside 8 feet= 4 points
Hole out = 6 points

Test three. Set up 50 yards from your target. Pitching or sand wedge.
8-15 feet = 1 point
Inside 8 feet = 4 points
Hole out = 6 points

Test four. Set up 35 yards from your target. Use a pitching wedge or a sand wedge.
8-12 feet = 1 point
Inside 8 feet = 4 points
Hole out = 6 points

Now Do It!

Test five. 20-yard chip shot with the eight-iron. Fly the ball 1/3 of the way and let it roll 2/3 of the distance to the hole.
Inside 6 feet = 3 points
Hole out = 6 points

Test Six. 20-yard lofted shot with the sand wedge. Plan the shot so that the ball flies approximately 2/3 of the distance in the air and rolls the rest of the way.
Inside 8 feet = 3 points
Hole out = 6 points

Test Seven. 15-yard lob wedge. Fly the ball high, land it three or four yards short of the hole, and let it roll the rest of the way.
Inside 6 feet = 2 points
Hole out = 6 points

Test Eight. 10-yard chip shot. This is the easiest shot on the test. You'll hole some. Land the ball on the green and let it roll most of the way. Use an eight or nine-iron.
Inside 4 feet = 2 points
Hole out = 6 points

Test Nine. 25-yard greenside bunker shot. Sand or lob wedge. Control distance with length of backswing.
Inside 12 feet = 3 points
Hole out = 6 points

Test Ten. 10-yard greenside bunker shot. Sand or lob wedge. Control distance with length of your backswing.
Inside 8 feet = 2 points
Hole out = 6 points

Make Your Golf Dream A Reality

Compare your results with those below, based on five balls per test (double the numbers for the ten-ball test).

Scratch and better	80+
Single digit handicap	65-79
10-15 handicap	50-64
16-20 handicap	35-49
High handicap	below 35

****

Make a copy of page 127 and put these Pre-round Reminders in your car. Review them before you step onto the course. You'll play better.

Now Do It!

Pre-round Reminders

1. On full shots, keep your right shoulder back and low, with your head behind the ball.
2. Monitor ball position in your stance. Guard against placing the ball too far forward or back, and too close or too far from your body.
3. Keep your weight on the inside of your right foot, with the right heel rotated slightly away from the target. This allows you to turn your body against a solid right leg on the backswing.
4. Practice and feel the Post Impact Position four or five times before play.
5. Check your grip—Vs pointed to the right ear and two knuckles visible on each hand.
6. Swing Medicus/Refiner and Momentus clubs for a few minutes.
7. Use impact tape to check your impact point.
8. Align every golf shot, practice or play, with a ground spot in front of the ball.
9. Before you swing, align feet, hips, and particularly shoulders with the target line.
10. On full swings, keep your right ear lobe perfectly still until the right shoulder brings your head up.
11. Swing at 80 percent of full power.
12. Make good balance a part of every shot, from the drive to the putt.
13. Grip lower on the club when playing short shots around the green.
14. When you putt, move *nothing* except your arms and shoulders. Allow the putter to release through the ball.
15. Be conservative, but not fearful. Play to make the next shot easy. Your primary job is to minimize blowup holes.
16. Focus on the process. Realize that you don't die from bad golf shots. Relax and choose shots that match your abilities, swing freely, and enjoy the round.

Make Your Golf Dream A Reality

To Become a Real Golfer You Must:

1. Understand where your game is weak and spend at least sixty to seventy-five hours per year in focused practice, improving these weak areas.
2. Know how to correctly line up and aim a golf shot.
3. Play from the right tees for your distance and drive the ball well enough to hit the fairway half or more of the time.
4. Recognize when you're stuck and need to take a lesson from a professional.
5. Hit five to ten greens in regulation per eighteen holes.
6. Average no more than about 32 putts per round, and strive for 30 or fewer.
7. Have at least nine reliable short game shots for known distances from thirty-five to one hundred yards (3x3 system or 3x4 system).
8. Pitch and chip the ball all the way to the hole on the first attempt and get it close enough to one-putt five to eight times per eighteen holes.
9. Be able to get out of a greenside bunker and make an occasional par, and seldom worse than bogey.
10. Think your way around the course and play safely enough to minimize blowup holes.
11. Play with due respect for the golf course, but without unreasonable fear.

Now Do It!

Rate Yourself

On each of the skills listed below, rate yourself often. If you're honest with yourself, you'll know exactly what's costing you strokes. Identify your weakest link and resolve to improve that aspect of your game. Don't use all of your practice time on one part of your game, but give it enough attention to get it off the bottom rung of the ladder.

Don't fall into the trap of constantly working on "the swing." No more than one-third of your practice time should be devoted to full swing shots. It's better to concentrate on proper setup before the swing takes place. Set aside time every month for practice on chipping, pitching, putting, and particularly distance control with the wedges – not hours a day, but a few hours each month. The mark of a true golfer is expertise in controlling distance from within one hundred yards of the green.

Rate Yourself in These Areas

1. Correct setup and aim
2. Distance control wedges (thirty-five to one hundred yards)
3. Pitch shots (ten to thirty-five yards)
4. Chipping
5. Sand play
6. Putting
7. Driver and full swing shots (no more than one-third of practice time)
8. Fearless, but smart and conservative play

14

Final Thoughts

As my golf game was getting better, I always looked forward to learning new shots and techniques. I didn't over-practice, but I tried to spend several hours every month on my game. I saw practice not as drudgery, but as opportunity. When I'd stand on the practice range, 50 or 60 yards from a green and stick a couple of balls close to the flagstick, I'd think to myself, "Yes! I can't wait to use this shot on the course."

It's easy to fall into a routine of playing, working on "the swing," playing, working more on "the swing," playing, working still more on "the swing," and getting nowhere. My training consisted of trying to make sure that I always picked a target, that I used an aim club, and that I was set up correctly before I ever started a backswing. That's a big part of the full swing battle in itself.

Final Thoughts

Don't mindlessly beat balls on the range. As with everything else in golf, you don't have to be perfect, just pretty good. 150 range shots every week – each with correct setup and aim to a specific target, are plenty for any high handicapper trying to get better. Quality, not quantity, is what matters most.

If your heart's only desire is to pull out the driver and knock your ball into the next county, don't keep score, forget about keeping a handicap, and don't bet. Plan instead on spending a good part of your life searching for lost balls. That's not golf.

If you want to be a real golfer, distance control wedges, pitching, chipping and lots of one-putts are the keys to your success. Without skill in the short game, your scorecard will continue to tell the same awful story. If you aren't recording at least five or six one-putts per round, your wedge game, pitching, and chipping need attention. Full swing training won't help.

Use whatever swing you've got today and apply what's in this book. Move to the correct tees for your length. Learn to set up and correctly aim a golf shot straight, no matter how strange it might feel. Continue until correct setup becomes a habit. That will bring out the best in your swing.

Get the ball all the way to the hole with your first pitch or chip. Be willing to accept bogey to keep blowup holes off your scorecard. Play to make the next shot easy. Take the short game handicap test often and work on your weakest areas.

When your game goes to pot, try not to be discouraged. If you can't figure out what's wrong, discuss your troubles with a professional and schedule a lesson. Take an occasional break and reread this book. It's short, and you'll soon forget a lot of what's here.

Don't get obsessed with all the different drills and instructions, trying to do everything at once. You have plenty of time to do everything in this book. Relax. Do as much as your schedule allows. Every hour of practice will pay future dividends. Your improvement will start right away, and if you stay with it, your game will soon turn completely around.

Finally, don't wear yourself out practicing. Golf is fun – never forget that. Be smart. Resolve to systematically address your weaknesses and dedicate sixty to seventy-five thoughtful hours each year to the ideas presented in this book. Stay positive and play plenty of golf, swinging freely and having a good time.

Many happy days at the golf course are in your future.

Glossary

Approach Shot–a shot intended to land on the green.

Birdie–a score of one under par on a single hole.

Blowup Hole–a badly played hole, several strokes above par.

Bogey–a score of one over par on a single hole.

Carry–the distance a golf ball flies before hitting the ground.

Charge (a putt)–hitting a putt hard enough to hold a line, but with the risk of the ball going well past the hole if it misses.

Chip Shot–a short, low running shot on the green, usually hit from within a few yards of the putting surface.

Chunk–hitting the ground behind the ball before hitting the ball itself, normally leading to loss of distance.

Deloft–moving the hands left at address, decreasing the loft of a club and producing a lower shot.

Double Bogey–a score of two over par on a single hole.

Double Eagle–a score of three under par on a single hole (the rarest shot in golf). Referred to as "Albatross" in Britain.

Draw–a golf shot that moves gently from right to left.

Drop–the manual repositioning of a golf ball, usually from an unplayable position. A drop typically involves a penalty.

Eagle–a score of two under par on a single hole.

Fade–a golf shot that moves gently from left to right.

Fat Shot–hitting the ground behind the ball before hitting the ball itself, causing loss of distance.

Get Down–Get the ball into the hole.

Green in Regulation–placing your ball on the green in one stroke on a par three, two strokes on a par four, and three strokes on a par five.

Hacker–a bad golfer.

Handicap–the number of strokes above or below par a golfer would be expected to shoot on an average of the best ten of his or her last twenty rounds.

Hole Out–knocking the ball in the hole.

Hook–a golf shot that moves wildly from right to left.

Lag–a conservative putt, hit with the idea of leaving the ball within easy one-putt range.

Lay up–intentionally hitting the ball to a point short of maximum distance in order to leave an easy follow up shot.

Less Club–a club that hits the ball a shorter distance.

Loft–angle of the face of a golf club relative to the shaft.

Long Game–longer maximum distance golf shots.

More Club–a club that hits the ball a longer distance.

OB–out of bounds.

Par–the number of strokes (3, 4, or 5) that the scorecard suggests as an expert score for a particular hole. For a full length 18-hole course, par is usually 70 to 72 strokes.

Pin High–an approach shot that flies the correct distance (even with the flagstick), but to the left or right.

Pitch Shot–a short, high shot, usually 35 yards or shorter, that lands and stops quickly on the green.

Pull–a straight golf shot that goes to the left.

Punch Shot–a low flying golf shot, normally the result of a delofted club and less than a full swing.

Push–a straight golf shot that goes to the right.

Scramble–a team event, usually 2 to 4 golfers, in which each player tees off and the best shot is selected, after which all golfers play their second shot from that spot. The best of those shots is selected, etc. continuing until the ball is holed.

Short Game–golf shots hit from less than 100 yards of the hole.

Short Sided–the result of an approach shot missing the green on the same side as the flag, leaving a difficult chip or pitch shot with little green between the ball and the flagstick.

Skull–a low-running shot hit with the bottom of the clubface that travels a much greater distance than intended.

Slice–a golf shot that moves wildly from left to right.

Stroke and Distance Penalty–loss of a stroke hit plus one penalty shot, and loss of the distance the ball traveled–in effect, a punishment of two shots. For example, a drive hit out of bounds leaves the golfer still on the tee and hitting his *third* shot. This punitive rule is extremely unpopular with golfers.

Sucker Pin–a flagstick placed near the edge of a green with danger nearby.

Triple Bogey–a score of three over par on a single hole.

Up and Down–getting the ball in the hole in two shots, the first usually from near the green onto the green (up), the second, holing the putt (down).

Index

Index

Index

About the Author

Lou Hays was a pioneer in the desktop publishing revolution. A twenty-year tournament chess expert, he founded Hays Publishing in 1990. The company produced more than twenty popular books on chess over a decade, including all-time bestseller, *My System–21st Century Edition.*

In the late 90's, Hays discovered the joys of golf, devoted himself to the game and soon became a first-rate player. A desire to tell his story and explain his unique system of golf improvement led to the publication of *Make Your Golf Dream A Reality.*

He and his wife, Susan, make their home on the banks of the Illinois River near Tahlequah, Oklahoma.

Quick Order Form

For purchase of additional copies of
Make Your Golf Dream A Reality

Fax orders: 918-456-7737. Fill out and send this form.

Online orders: www.hayspub.com (No "e" in Hays) Master or Visa

Mail orders: Hays Publishing, PO Box 777, Park Hill, OK 74451, USA

Please send _____ copies of *Make Your Golf Dream a Reality* at $13.9 each. I understand that I may return any book for a full refund.

Name: _____

Address: _____ _____

City: _____State: _____ Zip: _____

Country _____

Telephone _____

Email address: _____

Shipping:

U.S.: $4.00 first book, $2.00 for each additional book to same address.

International (air): $8.00 (US) for first book; $4.00 for each additional book to same address.

Visa or Master Number:

_____Expiration: _____/_____

Signature of cardholder _____